THE
WORLD'S
SECRET
POLICE

THE WORLD'S SECRET POLICE

BRUCE QUARRIE

OCTOPUS BOOKS

First published in 1986 by
Octopus Books Limited
59 Grosvenor Street, London W1

© 1986 Octopus Books Limited

ISBN 0 7064 2267 8

Made and printed in Great Britain by
Richard Clay (The Chaucer Press) Limited, Bungay, Suffolk

CONTENTS

CHAPTER ONE

'WE HAVE WAYS...'
SECRET POLICE AROUND THE WORLD TODAY

Mention the words 'secret police' to the average person and he will respond 'Gestapo' in nine cases out of ten. Certainly the *Geheime Staatspolizei* was one of the most ruthless, pitiless, brutal and inhumane organizations ever conceived by man. Its wartime exploits against the Jews, against resistance fighters in Nazi-occupied territories, against ethnic and religious groups elsewhere and, of course, against Allied agents, are well known. The Gestapo's principal tool was terror. Intimidation, beatings, torture, threats to the families of suspects and ultimate consignment to the firing squad or an extermination camp were its weapons.

The Gestapo, fortunately, is history. This book, however, is about secret police forces in the world today, and I hope sincerely that the horror and terror that they cause will appall all my readers in the same way that they did me, once I started researching the subject. To put it in a nutshell, there is not one continent in the world today free of at least one secret police force as ruthless, if not more so, as the Gestapo. By the time you have read this page, somewhere, someone will have been executed; someone else will have had electrodes applied to the most sensitive parts of his body; someone will have been arrested off the street or been dragged out of bed in the middle of the night for a journey to an unknown interrogation centre; someone will have been raped by police guards; someone will have been injected with a harmful drug; someone will be hanging by his ankles from the ceiling prior to being beaten with pickaxe handles, rubber truncheons or wire whips. By the time you finish reading this book, dozens, if not hundreds of people, somewhere in the world, will be enduring similar agonies.

When I was first asked to write *The World's Secret Police*, I thought that the emphasis would be on the Russian KGB, the American CIA, the British Special Branch, the French SDECE and perhaps a few others, such as the secret police forces of Libya or El Salvador. It rapidly became apparent that keeping to this plan was not only impossible but would have resulted in a totally unbalanced book, because the principal villains among the secret police forces of the world today are those whom few people have heard of, yet whose excesses rival anything perpetrated by either the Gestapo or the NKVD under Stalin.

For the purposes of this book, I have omitted reference to the intelligence-gathering and counter-espionage duties which inevitably form a major part of the duties of any secret police force, since these are more appropriately discussed in a separate volume. Similarly, I have largely avoided reference to the special military outfits which work hand-in-hand with the security forces in the prevention of terrorism, for example, since these are covered in my earlier book, *The World's Elite Forces*. What I have concentrated upon is those secret police forces around the world whose principal target is the people of their own nations.

The regimes discussed range from communist to fascist and include some so-called democracies. What they almost all have in common is a government which is so disliked by so many of its people that it can only maintain power by force. Exceptions are those countries which include ethnic minority groups seeking self-determination against the wishes of the ruling or occupying power, or similar religious groups looking for freedom of observance. In some instances it has been necessary to delve back many years into a country's history to explain how and why the present circumstances have arisen; in other cases — such as Iran, for example — internal terrorism is a very recent phenomenon.

I defy anyone to finish reading this book feeling neither unmoved nor angry. I have quoted verbatim from many first-hand accounts of people who have miraculously survived secret police maltreatment and torture, and I hope that these testimonies bring to life the dismal statistics of numbers of people imprisoned or killed for 'political offences' around the world in recent years. Finally, I would like to say that any errors of fact or omission in this book are mine alone and no fault of anyone who has helped me in its writing.

* * *

It would have been impossible to write this book without the tremendous help afforded by Rob Freer, press officer of the UK branch of Amnesty

International, whose headquarters are in the City of London. Amnesty International is a world-wide, apolitical organization whose concern is the treatment of prisoners of conscience and the abolition of the death penalty everywhere. It has over half a million members in more than 150 countries and bases its activities upon the United Nations Universal Declaration of Human Rights. Due to certain press coverage, Amnesty International is often thought of as a 'left-wing' organization. This is not true, although those of the 'right' may disagree with the organization's stand against the death penalty for those convicted of using violence for political ends. The organization summarizes its own aims and activities succinctly as follows:

'It seeks the *release* of men and women detained anywhere for their beliefs, colour, sex, ethnic origin, language or religion, provided they have not used or advocated violence.

'It advocates *fair and early trials for all political prisoners* and works on behalf of such persons detained without charge or without trial.

'It opposes the *death penalty* and *torture* or other cruel, inhuman or degrading treatment or punishment of *all prisoners* without reservation.'

Those interested in learning more about AI's work should write to:

Australia – Australian Section, PO Box No A159, Sydney South, NSW 2000.

Canada – Canadian Section (English-speaking), 294 Albert Street, Suite 204, Ottawa, Ontario K1P 6E6, or (French-speaking), Section Canadienne, 1800 Boulevard Dorchester ouest, Suite 127, Montréal, Quebec H3H 2H2.

United Kingdom – British Section, 5 Roberts Place, off Bowling Green Lane, London EC1 OEJ.

United States of America – 322 Eighth Avenue, New York, NY10001.

If you live elsewhere and would like to be put in contact with your local branch, you can obtain the address from the author c/o the publishers. Amnesty International publishes many books, reports and newsletters of its own giving the latest information on such subjects as political 'disappearances', torture, political killings and on the situation in different individual countries from time to time, all of which make compulsive reading.

CHAPTER TWO

THE UNITED STATES OF AMERICA

America might well be called the country which never wanted a secret police force, which has tried to do away with it by both public and private means ever since it was created, yet which continues to suffer its machinations daily.

Prior to World War Two, the USA did not have an intelligence service worthy of the name and relied upon information supplied by predominantly British sources. During the war a very efficient joint Services agency, the Office of Strategic Studies (OSS) was built up, but in the immediate post war aftermath it was run down until President Harry Truman, faced with the impossible task of deciphering intelligence reports from the army, navy, marines and air force, called for the creation of a National Intelligence Authority to centralize and collate the vast flow of information which landed on his desk every day. The NIA did not last long. Its task as briefed was impossible and it was still run and staffed by military consultants and advisors – and American politicians have long distrusted the armed services. Congress, therefore authorized the creation of a new, completely civilian security force, the Central Intelligence Agency, whose reports and activities were to be funnelled through the National Security Council which did and still does coordinate the efforts of the American military intelligence agencies as well as those of the Secret Service (which exists to protect the life of the incumbent President, his advisors and visitors), the Treasury Department, the Internal Revenue, Customs, Immigration and other government bodies, including the Federal Bureau of Investigation or FBI.

The first Director of the CIA was Allen Dulles: he was replaced after the Bay of Pigs affair in 1961 by John McCone, who was himself replaced after John Kennedy's assassination by Richard Helms; following Watergate it was William Colby . . . and so the story continues. Every time there is a government security scandal, domestic or overseas, it is the head of the CIA whose head goes on the block, and the operations of the agency have been so expressed in public debate and the media that it must be the least 'secret' secret police force in the world. Since January 1981 the Director has been William J. Casey.

Drive (or catch the bus) along the George Washington Parkway through the heavily wooded Virginia countryside alongside the River Potomac, and you would hardly know that the vast CIA headquarters complex lies at Langley — especially since they took the road sign down a few years ago. Turn off the Parkway on to a side road and the first of two chain-link fences, patrolled by inconspicuous guards and constantly scanned by normal and infra-red television cameras, greets you. In front is a massive modern white concrete and glass eight-storey building surrounded by car parks and helicopter pads, with hangars at the rear. Radio aerials cover the roof, but this is only the surface, for most of the complex lies underground; some of it deep enough to have a chance of withstanding a direct hit by a nuclear weapon. Inside, it is modern, clean, air-conditioned, and the security guards are unobtrusive, although everyone wears a badge and you require special authority to visit many areas. This is the home and HQ of the 20,000-odd people who make up the full-time establishment of the CIA. They include people from all walks of life, from the spies and sabotage experts of popular fiction to top experts with strings of degrees who specialize in economic, political and military intelligence analysis. Only a quarter of the CIA's personnel fit the public image of the agency. The rest are involved in management, in data processing and assessment, in translating and inter-preting foreign magazines, newspapers and radio and television broadcasts, in preparing maps and documents, and in what boils down to routine clerical office work. A high percentage of the agency's personnel hold degrees or doctorates and 20 per cent are fluent in three or more languages. But what does the CIA actually do?

When it was formed in 1947 the CIA was to undertake such tasks as might be required of it by the National Security Council in the interests of national security, but it was to have no hand in formulating policy and was prohibited from acting within the United States. It is largely fear that the last two criteria have been broached that has provoked the consecutive waves of criticism and investigation ever since the agency was established. The fear of an autonomous intelligence service only answerable to itself has been an American bogeyman for the last 40 years.

The CIA sees as its primary task the protection of American interests abroad and the prevention of the growth of communism, particularly in Latin America; rather as the KGB's overseas task is to halt — or reverse — the spread of capitalism. In the 1950s, therefore, the agency supported Carlos Castillo with arms and money in his guerrilla struggle against the Soviet-backed government of Arbenz Guzman in Guatemala. In Poland a CIA agent reported the departure of a ship loaded with arms from Czechoslovakia, ostensibly destined for Africa but in fact intended for Guatemala. The agency was powerless to stop the cargo arriving at Puerto Barrios, but ensured that Castillo's forces were supplied with sufficient modern weapons themselves to oust the government. The fact that Castillo's regime proved far more repressive and totalitarian than Arbenz's is a charge often laid at the CIA's doorstep, but except during the period when William Colby was Director, the agency has never replied to criticism any more than it has bragged in public about its successes.

One of its most resounding successes came shortly after the Guatemalan affair, when the CIA dug a tunnel from the American zone of Berlin into the east and tapped a vital communications cable capable of carrying up to 400 conversations or coded messages simultaneously. They operated the tap for a year before the tunnel was discovered. However, they then suffered a disaster in Iraq by failing to prevent the overthrow and murder of King Faisal. Chile was a more successful operation, although one which threw the agency into disrepute. A communist, Salvador Allende, narrowly won a general election in 1970 despite the substantial funds the CIA put into supporting his opponents. For the next three years the agency mounted a massive undercover campaign against him, pouring money into the country to create anti-Allende propaganda, to bribe the influential in the country's industries, to create a vast network of spies and informers, and generally to prepare the ground for his overthrow. The CIA was helped in this by large American businesses with heavy investments in Chile, particularly the International Telephone and Telegraph Corporation (ITT), and eventually a military junta took over the country in a bloody coup. The situation in Chile today is discussed elsewhere, but the CIA cannot feel proud of the regime they left in power, although they would 'justify' their actions as protecting American interests and preventing the spread of communism.

The agency had already come under fire for the celebrated 'Bay of Pigs' affair. Following Castro's take-over in Cuba, his increasingly violent anti-American statements and his increasing support from the Soviet Union, President Dwight D. Eisenhower had asked the CIA to draw up a plan to get rid of 'this madman'. Eisenhower lost the next election and John Kennedy became President in 1961, inheriting the CIA plan. Expatriate Cubans hostile to the Castro regime had been trained and equipped with modern weapons by the CIA. Mostly Catholics, they numbered 1,443 men

Headquarters of the Central Intelligence Agency, in Langley, Virginia.

and went under the name 'Brigade 2506'. A key ingredient in the plan was that the United States would launch at least three air strikes to destroy Castro's air force on the ground. Another was security, but Kennedy was worried by 'leaks' and the fact that the intended landing area for the invasion was widely reported in the media, so he changed it. Unfortunately, the region chosen was not only further from Havana than that originally selected, but was predominantly a deadly swamp. Moreover, Kennedy reduced the number of air strikes, leaving Brigade 2506 to be overwhelmed by Castro's Russian-supplied tanks and jet fighters. All of this was done apparently without the knowledge of either the CIA or the Joint Chiefs of Staff, but nevertheless Kennedy succeeded in pinning the blame on the agency and securing the resignation of Allen Dulles. If the original plans had been adhered to, it is more than likely that Castro would have been ousted from power and a pro-Western government reinstalled in his place.

It probably sounds from the foregoing as though the CIA operates principally in the interests of large American business, but in fact their involvement in both Chile and Cuba was part of an intensifying war — which continues today — against the KGB. Apart from internal repression, the KGB's principal function is to undermine and subvert all non-aligned governments using every means at its disposal, and it did not take long after the CIA's creation for it to become obvious that the agency had far more valuable work to perform than just acting as an intelligence clearing house. The KGB was — and is — 'the enemy', and the CIA has become a secret army whose chief aim is thwarting communist take-overs anywhere in the world. This does not of course mean that the CIA is invariably on the side of the 'good guys'. The Shah of Iran, whose own CIA-trained secret police force SAVAK eventually grew to three times the strength of the agency, who imprisoned tens of thousands of dissidents, and who regularly had political opponents executed as a matter of policy, only survived as long as he did because of the millions of dollars and the manpower poured into the country by the CIA. That the regime which has succeeded him is even more unpleasant could not have been predicted, but the fact that the CIA supported him is sure evidence that morality and politics rarely mix.

The CIA's worst blunder was to draw America into the Vietnam war, egged on by a Clandestine Services officer, Colonel (later General) Edward Lansdale who was convinced that America could win what proved to be a disastrous conflict. In Vietnam, the CIA operated much as the OSS had done during the Second World War, training and equipping groups of *montagnards* — the Civilian Irregular Defence Guards, or CIDG — and staging both amphibious and parachute commando-type raids deep behind enemy lines. The agency also operated its own air force which grew to some 500 aircraft (larger than many a national air force) engaged in bombing, in dropping agents and in electronic surveillance; and a small navy of spy ships. So secret were many of the agency's operations that not only were ships' names regularly changed, but aircraft serial numbers and code letters were repainted in between missions in order to preserve anonymity.

Today, CIA involvement in the affairs of other nations can be seen clearly. It was information supplied by the CIA which largely led to the invasion of Grenada in 1982, and it is CIA funding and arms supply which maintain the tension in El Salvador and Nicaragua. However, many people are more concerned with the agency's involvement in surveillance and other covert operations within the territorial United States. Despite its charter stating that it has no powers within the USA, this safeguard has steadily been eroded. First the CIA was allowed to question American citizens returning from trips abroad, then it was given similar powers to question foreign nationals living in the States. How far this erosion process has gone is the subject of constant — but unanswered — questions. Watergate sparked off the tidal wave of concern, when it emerged that at least two of those responsible for 'bugging' the Democratic National Committee headquarters — James McCord and Howard Hunt — were former CIA employees. However, William Colby, in his book *Honourable Men: My Life in the CIA* (Hutchinson), emphatically denies any CIA involvement, and considers that Richard Helms was dismissed by Nixon as a scapegoat in the same way that Dulles had been by Kennedy.

In situations like Watergate, one of the questions which continues to concern people is whether 'ex'-CIA personnel implicated are really 'ex' or simply taking leave of absence without pay while they do a job in which the agency would not like to be implicated if something comes unstuck. That this ploy is used regularly can be seen in the example of William Colby himself, who had been an active agent of OSS during the Second World War operating with the Resistance in both France and Norway. Afterwards, he stayed with the fledgling CIA — or Central Intelligence Group as it was first known when it was purely an information 'sorting office' — gradually rising through the ranks with post-war assignments in Scandinavia and Italy. He then spent some time in Vietnam, becoming a principal advisor and 'power behind the throne' to Ngo Dinh Diem's brother, Nhu. He returned to Washington to help organize the resistance in Laos to Viet Cong incursions: the 'secret war' to which Moscow turned a blind eye. Shortly afterwards, following the Tet offensive, which was a military failure for the Viet Cong but became a propaganda victory for them in the States, Colby went back to Vietnam. He took leave without pay and allowed himself to be 'hired' by the Agency for International Development (AID), which assigned him to a job with the Civilian Operations Revolutionary Development Staff (CORDS). The aim of this strangely and ambiguously named organization was to 'pacify' the villages and secure them from Viet Cong incursions, and

CORDS did not mind what methods it used — from providing schooling and medical care to supplying the most modern arms and expert instructors for local defence volunteers. There was a hidden side to the pacification programme (code-named 'Phoenix') and this was to hunt down and kill or imprison active or passive Viet Cong terrorists and sympathizers. For all that Colby issued a directive that American personnel involved in Phoenix were 'specifically not authorized to engage in assassinations or other violations of the rules of land warfare', it subsequently emerged that some 20,000 people, many of them unquestionably innocent of any terrorist activity, had been killed during the village pacification programme. The majority may well have been killed in genuine military engagements (as Colby later claimed). But even if only ten per cent were killed coldly or 'while resisting arrest', it is a damning indictment of a supposedly peaceful organization which was in fact led, and had its policies determined covertly, by the CIA.

At home in America again, Colby became Director of the CIA and was in charge when, in 1974, the *New York Times* ran a major front-page feature denouncing the CIA for indulging in operations against anti-war and other left-wing groups and individuals within the USA. While the CIA remained silent, public pressure for the facts to be released mounted and eventually a commission of enquiry was appointed. This concluded that 'the CIA has engaged in some activities that should be criticized and not permitted to happen again. . . Some of the activities were initiated or ordered by Presidents. . . Some of them were plainly unlawful.' Precise details of what was meant by these words are unknown, and likely to remain so for a long time, but the result was a 'spring clean' within the agency which has still not dispersed public distrust (especially abroad), and a continuing media scrutiny which has made covert CIA operations much more difficult to conduct. That this has been a good thing in terms of making the average American citizen freer of surveillance is undoubtedly true; but that it has made more difficult the CIA's principal task of counteracting Soviet (and especially KGB) operations is also true.

Former Deputy Director of the CIA, Admiral Bobby Inman.

CHAPTER THREE

LATIN AMERICA

ARGENTINA. BOLIVIA AND BRAZIL. CHILE. COLOMBIA. EL SALVADOR. GUATEMALA. OTHER COUNTRIES

Never politically stable, the countries of Central and South America have laboured for decades under a rapid succession of coups d'état, repressive military regimes and fascist civil governments. Most countries have severe economic problems and are beset with internal difficulties produced by the class structure which emerged during the 19th century. Because of resistance and the emergence of left-wing movements — whether democratic or communist in inspiration — every government in Latin America has been forced to create secret police forces to keep the population terrorized. In many countries, particularly Chile, El Salvador and Guatemala, life today is little different to what it was like in many occupied nations under Nazi rule, and there seems little prospect for radical change despite the efforts of the United Nations and human rights organizations such as Amnesty International. Behind the glittering façade of the cities which attract hundreds of thousands of tourists annually, lies a dim shadow world of violence in which kidnappings, torture and murder are daily occurrences.

Argentina
Until the military junta which had ruled the country since 1976 was deposed in the internal recriminations which followed the military campaign in the Falkland Islands during 1982, Argentina had for many years — indeed, decades — possessed one of the worst records for human rights violations

in the world. Political killings, 'disappearances' and the use of torture by both the police and the armed forces, either in order to extract 'confessions' and information or simply for punishment, were the order of the day and anyone with the vaguest left-wing affiliations lived in constant fear of sudden arrest. Today, under President Alfonsín, a more liberal attitude appears to be emerging, and in September 1984 Argentina signed the American Convention on Human Rights and recognized the jurisdiction of the Inter-American Court of Human Rights. However, there is still cause for concern, and the country's political future is unclear.

Like most Latin American countries, Argentina has seen a succession of different governments and military coups throughout the 20th century. Prior to the Second World War, the regime of President Ortiz and Dr Castillo was decidedly pro-German and similar in political outlook. As in all South American countries, there was an unequal class structure with the wealthy and educated men and women of European descent at the top and the Indians — whose population had been severely decimated during the 19th century — at the bottom. Ortiz died in 1942 and on 4 June the following year a military coup deposed Dr Castillo, who was succeeded by General Ramírez and then General Farrell, who severed diplomatic relations with Germany and Japan and, in March 1945, declared war on the Allied side. The period of respite from repression was short-lived however. Throughout the pre-war years an urbanized, industrial working class had grown up in Argentina, despite the fact that the country's principal source of revenue was beef and wool exports. Such people were not hugely interested in constitutional liberties or political freedom, or in the means by which any government held power, so long as the ruling party or individual served their own material interests. Riding to power with the support of this element of the population were two of the most significant Argentinian political personalities of the century, Colonel Juan Domingo Perón and his wife, Eva (née Duarte).

Perón, who was born in 1895, received German-inspired military training, and from 1939 to 1941 was Argentina's military attaché in Italy, where he developed a strong admiration for Mussolini. Perón was an ideal candidate for the hard-line Army *Grupo de Oficiales Unidos* and became head of the department of labour and social security in Ramírez' government, in which position he inevitably developed close links with the special intelligence division of the police known as the *Seccion Especial de Repression del Comunismo* (SERC).

Perón played his hand well, ably aided by his wife, who was always his best publicist. (The life of Eva Perón formed the basis for the popular musical *Evita*, from which one of the songs — *Don't Cry For Me Argentina* leaped into the hit parade during the Falkland Islands' conflict.) His support for the industrial working class of Argentina threw him into inevitable conflict with the older and more conservative elements in Ramírez' and Farrell's governments, a conflict which came into the open in October 1945 and led to elections in February 1946 which resulted in Perón becoming President. His main weapons once in power were the CERT and the *Confederación General del Trabajo* (CGT), the equivalent of Britain's Trades Union Congress. However, his attempts to increase the rate of industralization led to spiralling inflation, while his neglect of agriculture resulted in a drastic decline in Argentina's principal export industry. Three bad harvests between 1949 and 1951 ended in riots due to acute food shortages in the towns and cities. These caused Perón to clamp down even harder, and in 1951 he caused outrage by nationalizing the famous independent paper, *La Prensa*, putting total control of the media in his own hands. Although re-elected in 1951, Perón's grip on the country began to slacken after the death of his wife in July 1952, and in 1955 he was deposed and forced to flee into exile, first to Dominica and then to Spain, where he was made welcome by General Franco.

The following years saw rapid changes in the government of Argentina. Although the Perónist movement was officially banned, it remained covertly popular and in 1973 a Perónist candidate, Héctor Cámpora, was returned to power. Perón himself was invited home from exile and Cámpora handed over the reins of government to him for a short period until Perón's death in July 1974, when he was succeeded by his second wife, María Estela.

During his brief spell back in power, however, Perón had increased repressive measures against the left-wing groups — many of them by this time armed — which had sprung up during his period in exile and, using the *División de Información Politicas Antidemocráticus* (DIPA), which had replaced the old CERT, he began a reign of terror which was to continue after his death. Apart from the secret police, other unofficial right-wing groups came into being to whose activities the government turned a blind eye. These included the *Alianza Anti-comunista Argentina* (AAA) which, from the time of Perón's return to the presidency to the end of 1973, was responsible for at least 29 political killings; and the *Comando Libertadores de America* which had close military links. The latter organization rapidly assumed a great deal of power and, apart from conducting raids on left-wing political meetings, murdering opponents and terrorizing the civil population regardless of their political sympathies, was responsible for setting up the first forced labour camps — camps which were maintained by the military junta after 1976. Known as *La Perla*, these secret camps eventually grew to 47 in number and shared many similarities with the concentration camps of Nazi Germany.

One survivor of the camps was Graciela Geuna, who recently gave the following testimony.

'Before getting out of the lorry, the prisoners were tied up. They were

Argentinian parents protest the disappearance of their children.

then taken from the lorry and were forced to kneel in front of the trenches and then they were shot. I believe that these assassinations became a sort of military ceremony. Captain González also said that sometimes the officer in charge of the firing squad allowed the prisoners "five minutes" to pray. Sometimes they were told they were being executed for "treason". Those who were arrested while doing compulsory military service were shot wearing their uniforms.

'The bodies, riddled with bullets, lay in the trenches. They were then covered with an inflammable substance and burned.'

After the coup of March 1976 which overthrew Perón's second wife, the new military junta headed by President Videla launched an intensified military and police campaign against 'subversion'. The parliamentary Congress was dissolved and all the top positions in the judiciary were replaced by military appointments. The army was completely reorganized for the counter-insurgency role, control of 'subversive' elements being the direct responsibility of regional military commanders. Task forces were set up to capture and interrogate all known members of left-wing organizations, their sympathizers and associates. Normal legal procedures disappeared and abductions replaced formal arrests.

A report on a seminar organized by Amnesty International USA in 1980 states that 'a familiar pattern began to emerge. The victims were dragged from their homes at night by men who identified themselves as agents of the police or the armed forces. When relatives tried to find out what had happened by making enquiries at police stations or barracks and perhaps eventually filing writs of *habeas corpus*, they received no information or help . . . People captured alive by the military faced three possibilities. Their arrest might be acknowledged by the authorities and they might even be released after a brief detention, but usually prisoners were taken to a secret camp, not an officially recognized prison, belonging to the military or the police. There almost all were tortured and the majority were never seen again. Often, after being told that they were due to be "transferred", they were taken away and secretly executed.'

At least 5,000 people abducted between 1975 and 1981 have never been seen again.

Torture in the camps run by the military, by DIPA and by the CLA followed another familiar pattern. Detainees were usually interrogated during the early period of their arrest, when they were still in a state of shock and had not come to a fatalistic acceptance of their situation. Electric cattle prods were used to administer shocks to all parts of the body, including the genitals. Sacks soaked in water were placed over prisoners' heads. Beatings were commonplace, with rifle butts and truncheons being used in addition to fists and feet. Lighted cigarettes were applied to prisoners' skin. Sensory deprivation, lack of food and water, and forcing inmates to stand for long periods in awkward positions were further 'refinements'.

In 1979 the ruling junta introduced new legislation in response to increasing pressure both from the relatives of people who had disappeared and from international rights groups. This new measure was designed to cover up the real situation and make 'missing persons' investigations almost impossible. Called the Law on Presumption of Death Because of Disappearance, it made any missing person legally dead until proved alive — a complete reversal of any normal procedure in civilized countries.

One person who 'disappeared' was Rosa Ana Frigerio, who had been recovering from a serious spinal operation at her parents' home in Mar del Plata. She was encased in plaster from her waist to her knees, and was simply 'missing' when her parents returned home one day. To begin with, her parents were told that she had been taken to a naval hospital, but this was later denied. When her determined mother and father then courageously filed a writ of *habeas corpus*, they were informed that their daughter had been detained for indulging in 'subversive activities'. A month later they were summoned by a naval officer and told that Rosa Ana had been killed during a gunfight. The death certificate read 'cardiac arrest', the body had already been buried, and the parents were unable to obtain an exhumation order.

The bodies of many detainees ended up in the sea, since the Argentinian Navy was as involved in the 'disappearances' as the Army, police and paramilitary groups. The testimony of a survivor given in Madrid in 1980 reveals the following about the *Escuela de Macánica de la Armada*, or Naval School of Mechanical Engineering.

'Prisoners had to remain in the cells in silence. At approximately 5 pm each Wednesday people were selected for the transfer. They were led one by one to the infirmary just as they were, dressed or half-dressed, in hot or cold weather. In the infirmary they were given an injection, allegedly because hygiene conditions in the camps they were going to were very poor. In reality they were given a kind of sedative. Then they were taken by lorry to the *Aeroparque* [a military airfield] in Buenos Aires . . . and put on a Fokker airplane belonging to the Navy's multi-purpose air squadron. They would be flown out to sea towards the south to the point where the Gulf Stream would ensure the disappearance of the bodies. Then the prisoners were thrown alive out of the plane.'

Some bodies nevertheless were washed ashore. An Argentine coastguard, Victor González del Río, reported that 'you could see it was not a normal drowning . . . The dead bodies [he found ten] were, so far as one could see, in the 30-year-old age group. The corpses were usually mutilated by the fish. I think they had been drifting in the sea from a few days up to a few weeks. A number of corpses showed traces of ill-treatment, such as severed hands. Most corpses were naked, without rings, watches or neck-laces. Sometimes they wore underwear and in one case the body had been packed in a nylon bag.'

The coastguard was warned in no uncertain terms by the police to 'keep his mouth shut' and had it explained to him that the bodies had come from a sunken fishing boat. However, no boats, had been reported lost . . .

Today, following the events of 1982, the situation in Argentina is improving. The DIPA has been disbanded and in November 1983 the new government of President Alfonsín published a report entitled *Nunca Más* (Never Again) which catalogued no fewer than 8,960 unsolved 'disappear-ances' and warned that the actual total could well be higher. The report also disclosed the existence of 340 secret detention centres which had been used by the junta. In October 1984 the last 17 'political prisoners' still detained were released, and all those members of the military and police found guilty by due process of law (itself a lengthy affair) of having tortured prisoners under the junta received sentences ranging from five years to life imprisonment.

Nunca Más indeed.

The military policing the streets of Argentina.

Bolivia and Brazil

Compared to Argentina before the change of government in 1982, and to Chile today, the governments of both Bolivia and Brazil are reasonable in their treatment of 'political offenders' and 'subversives' — to reiterate those catchpenny phrases.

Bolivia had been a democracy since January 1980 until one of the typical Latin American coups established a military government later in the same year. This led to the predictable spate of arrests of journalists, trades union officials, civil rights leaders and students, mostly by the *Servicio Especial de Seguridad* (SES), or Special Security Service, but most detainees were released after relatively short incarcerations, provided they agreed to 'voluntary' exile abroad.

Rather than the SES, paramilitary organizations particularly those established by Colonel Luis Arce Gómez, the Minister of the Interior seem to have been principally responsible for the use of torture on prisoners. Their methods included those already described for Argentina with the additions of whipping, fingernail-pulling, and the insertion of nails or pins beneath the finger- and toe-nails.

Some 600 people are believed to have suffered from such treatment before the new government of President Hernán Siles Zuazo abolished the SES together with other security agenices such as the *Departamento de Orden Politico* (DOP) and *Departamento de Inteligencia del Estado* (whose acronym is, appropriately, DIE). However, there is continuing concern over the present government's slackness in bringing those men responsible for human rights violations to trial. There is clear evidence of witness intimidation and Gómez, although charged with assassination and genocide alongside lesser crimes, remained unpunished at the time of writing.

Brazil has a democratic constitution which prohibits inhumane treatment of prisoners and detainees, and does not have a secret police service as such — where necessary this function is carried out by the military. During the 1960s and '70s the situation was far worse, and common criminals in addition to the poor, unemployed and Indians were routinely tortured. Victims even included children. A favourite device was binding a detainee's ankes to his or her wrists and then suspending the prisoner head-down by means of a rod passed beneath the knees — a form of torture which produces excruciating muscle cramps.

All security in Brazil at this time was co-ordinated by the National Intelligence Service (SNI) whose operational branch was the *Destacamento de Operações e Informações — Centro de Operações de Defesa Interna*, or regional Divisions of Intelligence Operations — Co-ordination of Internal Defence (DOI-CODI or simply CODI to most people). These units were composed of men from all three branches of the armed forces as well as police and members of right-wing paramilitary groups, and their organization formed the model for the Argentinian system. Each regional CODI had four sections, responsible respectively for logistical support, information analysis, interrogation and torture, and search and arrest.

The *modus operandi* of the last three sections — whose men vied with each other in obtaining the highest number of arrests and 'confessions' — was similar to that of secret police forces everywhere. Secrecy was paramount, so prisoners were always blindfolded and agents used pseudonyms amongst themselves. Victims were arrested, often in broad daylight, by anonymous men in plain clothes driving ordinary cars with civil (but untraceable) number plates. If there were witnessses to an arrest, they were intimidated with threats to their personal safety and that of their families, or on occasion arrested themselves for no better reason than that they happened to be in the wrong place at the wrong time.

Prisoners were taken to secret 'safe houses' for interrogation, usually under torture. A doctor was always supposed to be present during such sessions to ensure that victims were fit enough to stand up to the brutalities inflicted upon them, but, needless to say, many prisoners still died. When this happened, spurious certificates were prepared giving innocuous causes of death.

Such behaviour today is far less prevalent, especially in the cities, which are largely westernized, but in the remote rural areas arbitrary persecution of the native Indian population still takes place. The Roman Catholic Church which, together with the Brazilian Bar Association, trades unionists and journalists, particularly opposes political and racial oppression in Brazil, reported towards the end of 1984 that some 40 rural peasants had been shot by armed farmers. This type of 'vigilante' behaviour by unofficial and, in some cases, mercenary groups, is still known to continue, despite urgent representations to the government by internal and external rights movements. Similarly, reports of activity by police 'hit squads' armed with shotguns continue to appear following the murder of journalist Mario Eugénio de Oliviera — who was investigating them on behalf of the *Correio Braziliense* — in November 1984. To what extent such groups are operating with or without the government's tacit approval remains unclear.

That the military police (*Policia Militar*) still uses torture in an effort to persuade people to 'change their minds', however, is clearly borne out by the testimony of council official Raquel Cândido e Silva, who opposed their forcible removal of some 2,000 peasants from disputed land in Eldorado in March 1984. The military police arrested her and took her to the central police station in Porto Velho, where she was severely beaten by the doctor and four MPs. Moved to another police station, she was threatened with rape, beaten again, and had lighted cigarettes placed against her feet. Two months after her arrest she finally appeared in court where physical examination by another doctor revealed a dislodged kidney as a result of her ill-treatment. Despite continuing accounts such as this, however, all attempts to bring the culprits to justice meet with a stone wall of official denial.

Chile

'At one point, I realized that my daughter was in front of me. I even managed to touch her. I felt her hands. "Mummy, say something, anything to make this stop", she was saying. I tried to embrace her but they prevented me. They separated us violently. They took her to an adjacent room and there, there I listened in horror as they began to torture her with electricity — my own daughter! When I heard her moans, her terrible screams, I couldn't take any more. I thought I would go mad, that my head and my entire body were going to explode.'

Such treatment, meted out to a Chilean woman in only recent months, is typical of the brutality of the *Central Nacional de Informaciones* (CNI), the dreaded Chilean secret police.

Lucia Guillermina Morales, 48 years old, was a member of the national trades union coordinating body. She, and eight other union leaders, were all arrested at the same time — 11 o'clock at night.

Security police herd opponents of the regime in Chile from a bus.

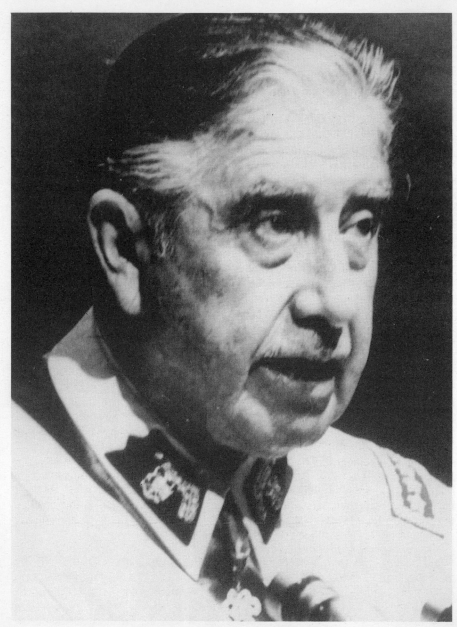

Chilean president General Augusto Pinochet Ugarte.

'Four men burst into the house. My daughter told them I was in bed but one of them came in and told me to get dressed. They were men in civilian clothes, armed to the teeth . . . they wore armbands and showed CNI identity cards. They did not produce any arrest or search warrant.

'They bundled me into a Peugeot 504 taxi and pushed me down on the floor. On arriving at the detention centre they made me take off all my clothes and put on an overall and lightweight shoes. Then I was given a medical examination and injected with a substance which they said was a tranquillizer.

'From the moment I arrived . . . they began to punch me about the head and slap me in the face. They avoided using their fists on my face so as not to leave any marks. They also hit me on the ears. I began to lose my sense of balance. Everything was spinning round. They shouted that I must confess to my political affiliations. "Confess you're a communist, you ****", they said. I don't know, I'm not well up on these things, but if I had an ideology of some kind I don't think I would want to hide the fact from anyone. Quite the opposite. But I would like to know why it is that just for thinking in a certain way one can be subjected to such atrocities.'

Mrs Morales was asked by a Chilean journalist three months after her arrest and eventual release what she did while she was being questioned.

'I kept quiet. I only did my best to answer their questions. They kept telling me they had 20 days to get the muck out of me and that no-one would notice anything when it was all over. "People have left here lame, or silly", they kept saying. Then they began to hurl all sorts of insults at me. They were very obscene. One of them asked what I thought they would do to me. I said I thought they would kill me. He answered that they didn't dirty their hands with women like me. Suddenly a nicer one came and told me that all they asked was that I behave myself and I would see they weren't the torturers people out there say we are. It was then that they told me that they were going to fetch my 23-year-old daughter Lucia.

'I became desperate, I screamed, I began to cry . . . the thought that my daughter would have to suffer what I had been through was intolerable . . . how can you describe what it means? On the next day they took me to a metal rack and made me lie on it, naked, tied at the wrists and ankles. With lead weights or electrodes they gave me electric shocks to the nipples, the stomach and the region of the vagina.'

It was at this point that Mrs Morales' daughter, Lucia, was brought in front of her and then tortured separately, though not so severely, in an adjacent room. After Mrs Morales gave her false confession she was sent into exile to a remote village on an island off Chile's coast for three months. Her subsequent charges of torture, and those of the other eight union officials similarly treated, were 'investigated' by the Military Prosecutor, who concluded that there was no evidence.

Chile is not a pleasant place in which to live. The present military government under General Augusto Pinochet Ugarde has been in power since a coup in 1973. It is rigid, autocratic and brooks no political opposition. Chile has suffered from economic and political problems throughout the century, being similar in many respects to Italy during the 1930s, then toying with a form of communism during the Second World War before a true form of democracy came into being during the late 1940s and '50s — Chile was the first Latin American country to grant women full political rights.

However, the country has always had to rely on imports to feed its population, paying principally in copper which is Chile's chief natural resource, and this, coupled with severe earthquake disasters, led to soaring inflation in the 1950s (156 per cent in two years). Stringent cuts in public spending, in an attempt to build up both agriculture and industry, led to considerable unrest from the trades unions and others throughout the 1960s. This situation eventually resulted in the military coup of 1973 which brought Pinochet to power, and which was followed by a wave of arrests and executions by the *Dirección de Inteligencia Nacional* (DINA), predecessor of the CNI which came into existence in 1977.

Thousands of people 'disappeared' following the coup — mostly political activists, trades unionists and the usual crop of impoverished and illiterate peasants who simply held land desired by the new ruling clique. As in Argentina, the work of the secret police was aided and abetted by semi-official paramilitary organizations such as the *Comando de Vengadores de Los Mártires* (COVEMA), or Avengers of the Martyrs, a covert fascist group principally composed of members of the military and security forces. One of their principal targets has been the illegal *Movimiento de Izquerida Revolucionaria* (MIR), or Movement of the Revolutionary Left, many of whose members have been forcibly abducted or even killed in public.

To begin with, DINA came into a certain degree of conflict with the intelligence services of the Chilean Air Force (SIPA) and Navy (SIN), since most of its recruits came from the Army (SIM) or the *Carabineros* (SICAR) but eventually — apart from port security which remains in the hands of SIN — DINA and its successor, the CNI, became responsible for all internal and external security in Chile. Disappearances, particularly among known communists and fellow-travellers, became widespread, but overt political resistance continued until the government declared a 'state of siege' in 1977 which continues to the present day. This effectively eliminated all normal legal procedures and safeguards, making arrest, detention, torture and murder feasible without the victims or their relatives having any chance of appeal. Pinochet went even further in 1978 when he promulgated his Decree Law on Amnesty, which gave a blanket pardon and immunity from arrest to all members of the security forces who might have committed crimes since his accession to power.

A tribute to the disappeared in Chile.

La parrilla — the metal rack referred to in Mrs Morales' testimony above — is one of the most common forms of torture employed by the Chilean secret police. The victim is strapped to a bare metal bed frame and electric shocks are administered to various parts of the body. An even more unpleasant variation is that in which — rather as in Brazil in the past — the prisoner is trussed like a turkey, legs bent and wrists strapped to ankles. A pole is then passed between the bent knees and elbows and the victim hung upside down – sometimes with his or her head in a pail of water – while similar electric shock treatment is administered. Drugs are also used by the CNI, and sexual abuse of female prisoners is rife.

The CNI today operates under Chilean law number 18.314, which purportedly defines terrorist conduct and establishes its penalties. Two articles of this give the secret police powers to arrest, detain and interrogate suspects without a warrant for up to ten days before they must be brought before a judge. In practice, even these wide powers are abused and many people known to have been arrested simply disappear: their fates can be imagined. Requests for investigation and trial of those responsible have simply been ignored by the military authorities.

A typical example of arbitrary arrest was that endured by philosophy student José Grossi Gallizia and a friend, Julio Araya Godoy, who were seized in the street early one evening in Santiago by two armed plainclothes policemen. After being forced to lie face-down on the pavement while they were searched, the pair were handcuffed and driven away in a red Chevrolet Opala, via the house of a friend they had been visiting, to a *Carabineros* station. After being asked the type of police questions that are routine everywhere, and being photographed, they were blindfolded and left standing for several hours. They were then transferred to another location — still blindfolded until their arrival.

José Grossi takes up the narrative at this point.

'On arrival we were taken to a room with vinyl armchairs and a TV set that was switched on. Shortly afterwards we were transferred to another room which I managed to get a glimpse of; it was light green with doors and doorframes and had a small photo of Pinochet hanging on a wall. There were metal desks and a metal card-index. There, after an intimidatory talk, someone urged us to talk, as afterwards it would be the turn of the specialists. Sure enough, the specialists did arrive. There were at least three of them, one who asked questions in a refined voice and two others who were less refined and who administered the torture in accordance with the first man's instructions.

'When these people appeared, Julio Araya was removed from the room. I found myself handcuffed and seated on a chair with my hands behind my back, with a blindfold covering my eyes and a hood over my head. During the interrogation I was given electric shocks; for this purpose a wire had been connected to my handcuffs, while a hard object was used to give me electric shocks to the abdomen, the palms of my hands and the base of my right thumb. The voltage was increased to the point where at times my body shook violently and I had to be firmly held by one of the people who was torturing me . . . [I] at one point gave one of them a kick as I felt a violent electric discharge in the stomach which left me unable to move and suffering from convulsions.'

On this occasion the police must have realized eventually that they had picked up innocent suspects. By about midnight — Grossi could hear the television channel closing down — the torture stopped. However, the two men were left handcuffed back-to-back, with hoods over their heads, until the following morning when they were given coffee then driven around the city for a couple of hours in a closed van before being dropped off, still blindfolded, in one of the main streets.

Others have not been so lucky. In September 1984 Juan Aguirre Ballesteros was arrested and taken to a police station where he was similarly tortured by means of electric shock treatment. The authorities denied that he was in their hands, and he was listed as 'missing' until the middle of the following month when his headless and mutilated body was discovered dumped in a street. Another such victim was Mario Fernández López, a member of the Christian Democrat Party, who died in hospital from internal injuries a day after having been arrested and severely beaten by two CNI men. An attempt was actually made to try to prosecute the pair by a civil court but, because the CNI are considered part of the military, the case was referred to a military judge who dismissed it on the grounds of insufficient evidence.

Doctors, teachers and lawyers — those with the intelligence and education to know that things are wrong and who have the courage to stand up and say so — are also prime targets for the CNI today. Strikers, and those attempting to take part in political rallies, are often killed in uncontrolled shoot-outs which also result in the deaths of innocent children.

The Chilean government has made no response to the appeals and demands for investigations made by organizations such as Amnesty International, and life in Chile today remains tragically similar to that under the Gestapo in occupied Europe during the Second World War.

Colombia

Conditions in Colombia have improved enormously in the last couple of years since President Belisario Betancur offered dissident guerrilla groups a truce, at the beginning of 1984. Unfortunately this was not entirely to the liking of criminal drug-traffickers, who had been benefiting from the state of internal disorder which was tying down both the police and the military, and armed unrest continued throughout the rest of the year until all guerrilla groups with the exception of the Marxist *Ejército de Liberación Nacional* (ELN), or National Liberation Army, finally agreed to a cease-fire. Meanwhile, murders and disappearances still continue, most of them being attributed to the officially denounced *Muerte a Secuestradores* (MAS) (Death to the Sequestrators) death squad which was originally formed as an anti-kidnapping vigilante-style unit but which the government now finds useful for covert operations in which it can deny having had a hand.

Until 1982, Colombia, northernmost country of South America, had a human rights problem rivalled by few. Its right-wing government was violently opposed by large numbers of people from all walks of life, including peasant farmers and university intellectuals, who formed many resistance groups, most of them armed. To counter this the government had the army and police intelligence services, known simply as B-2 and F-2 respectively. Suspects were arrested, usually without formality, and taken to detention centres for an interrogation period which usually lasted from five to ten days. The techniques used will by now be familiar to readers of this book — prisoners were stripped naked and blindfolded then subjected to systematic beatings, immersion in water, electric shock treatment, sexual abuse and lack of food, water or sleep; drugs were also used.

When the secret police methods began to be questioned openly as a matter of urgent public debate in Colombia during the early 1980s, the number of arrests — particularly in the cities — declined noticeably, but ill-treatment of suspects in the remote rural areas continued. Less sophisticated interrogation techniques were needed here: it was usually found sufficient to bind a prisoner to a tree or post, exposed to the fierce sun during the day, to insects at dusk and to freezing cold at night. Alternatively, a prisoner could be suspended by his or her arms from a convenient tree branch and used as a punchball by soldiers wielding rifle butts instead of fists.

Most of the victims of such treatment were Indians suspected of cooperating with one or another of the active guerrilla groups. However, in many cases such accusations were pure inventions contrived to drive the peasant farmers from their land — a scenario which will be familiar to watchers of 'Westerns'. Since 1984 many such abuses have been investigated by the Colombian Attorney General, especially those perpetrated by members of the Army Intelligence Brigade (*Brigada de Institutos Militares*, or BIM) in Bogotá. At least 11 farmers are known to have been killed by this organization in April 1984, provoking the comment from the Attorney General that 'the country has not taken seriously the policy of defending human rights'.

El Salvador
'Thirty heavily armed men wearing army combat vests, but masked and with hoods lettered death squad came to my village and seized and killed

a number of *campesinos* (peasants). They went then to the neighbouring village of Santa Helena, scizcd Romilia Hernandéz, aged 21, raped and then decapitated her. Her relatives buried her head; the rest of her body was burned by her murderers. The head had been left in front of her relatives' house. The members of the death squad were evacuated that day by a Salvadorean army helicopter.'

So runs part of the testimony from just one of thousands of refugees from El Salvador, a country in which Archbishop Arturo Rivera y Damas claims 11,723 innocent people were murdered by the government in 1981 alone. This situation is not new and dates back to at least 1962 when a paramilitary unit named the *Organización Democrática Nacionalista* (ORDEN) was formed by Colonel Alberto Medrano, an army officer rumoured at the time to have also been head of military intelligence in El Salvador. For five years Medrano built up his organization, recruiting from both the military and the civilian population, into a significant force for intimidation and repression. After ORDEN helped Colonel Fidel Sanchez Hernandez become President in 1967, its powers were increased and it had secret government support and funding, control over its activities being

Uniformed officers kill two schoolboys in San Salvador.

exercised by the army. However, President Sanchez feared that it could become a private army like Himmler's SS in Nazi Germany, and eased Medrano out, assuming ultimate responsibility for the organization himself. In the 1970s control passed to Sanchez' successor, President Carlos Humberto Romero, by which time the organization had grown to an estimated strength of 80,000 to 100,000 men, with a probable reserve in time of emergency of a further 50,000 to 70,000. What sort of people are these? In 1979 an Associated Press report stated that 'generally the members of ORDEN are people that live in conditions of extreme misery, who in order to keep afloat with the help of the government become members of the organization. . . . Others join ORDEN to keep their jobs in the government or to better themselves in their employment; others to ingratiate themselves with the agents of the security forces; others to have influence in politics; others to live almost like policemen; others because the ORDEN identification card permits them to live arrogantly and commit any kind of abuse.'

Official security services in El Salvador are the National Guard, the National Police and the Treasury Police, supported by the CIA-trained Atlactl Brigade, a counter-insurgency unit for use principally in the field

Trying to identify those killed during FDN night operations.

Demonstrators protest against disappearances in El Salvador.

against armed guerrilla groups. As far as the general population is concerned, however, ORDEN — renamed *Frente Democrático Nacionalista* (FDN) after the latest military coup d'état in 1979 — is still the organization to be really feared. Tens of thousands of people have 'disappeared' or been brutally killed, like Romilia Hernandez, in the last few years under the pretext of combating communism. Principal targets of the FDN are students and university staff, trades unionists, liberal politicians and human rights workers, both national and international, whose efforts meet with constant harassment and short-term imprisonment.

Recent examples of the FDN's work are the fates of Dr José Guillermo Orellana Osorio and Dr Juan Francisco Aguirre, both members of the National University's Faculty of Law. Dr Osorio was kidnapped from his office at the university by plain-clothes men in October 1983; his body was 'found' three weeks later — he had been tortured and strangled. Dr Aguirre was arrested while leaving a class at the end of the following month; he has never been seen since.

Torture methods used by the security forces in El Salvador — who frequently cross the border into neighbouring Honduras to track down and seize Salvadorean refugees — include the usual beatings, sexual abuse of women and so on, with the addition of the use of drugs and chemicals to produce disorientation, and concentrated sulphuric acid to produce agonizing burns right down to the bone. The country's current President, Napoleón Duarte, shows no inclination to halt such practices despite recriminations from the United Nations General Assembly. Other known killings by the Salvadorean security forces documented in Amnesty International's latest annual report include those of Archbishop Oscar Romero and American journalist John Sullivan, as well as the massacre of 74 peasants in Sonsonate. Another 70 villagers were killed by the Atlactl Brigade (which is actually believed to be of about battalion size, ie 600–700 men) in July 1984. In the same year a Lutheran pastor, the Reverend David Ernesto Fernández Espino, was arrested by two armed men. His body was later found having been mutilated by a machete: he had been shot through the head. Similarly, a lecturer at the Roman Catholic University, Reynaldo Echevarría, was shot one evening as he arrived home by a plain-clothes official in an unmarked car.

In January 1984, 14 trades unionists were arrested at a convention. Among them was a Mexican observer who was later released. She testified that she had been blindfolded and subjected to 'intense psychological pressure' during her three-day internment, and said that she could hear other prisoners being beaten, while conditions in the National Police Headquarters were appalling, with 15 to 20 people being packed into cells designed for two. Following her testimony, pressure from the UN secured the release of the other prisoners, all of whom claim to have been tortured in an attempt to extract confessions that they were members of an armed opposition group. Similar happenings are still an everyday occurrence.

Guatemala

Anyone wishing to understand today what life was like under Stalin's NKVD or Hitler's Gestapo will find a visit to the Guatemalan 'Republic' an informative exercise — but they should ensure that sufficient influential friends know where they are before attempting any detailed investigation of the methods employed by either the army or the *Ejército Secreto Anti-Comunista* (ESA); a paramilitary undercover organization backed by successive governments since the late 1970s, whose aims are the destruction of any vaguely liberal or left-wing groups in the country.

Guatemala is, and has been since the mid-1960s, one of the most outright fascist and repressive regimes in the world, and the list of atrocities perpetrated by the internal security forces in the name of 'law and order' has few rivals. Because Guatemala has served as a 'model' which many other Latin American states have striven to emulate, its history and the reasons for the present situation deserve closer examination. But first:

'The soldiers came; we went to the mountains; there we found tree trunks and stones where we hid. A group of soldiers came from behind, they came in behind us. They seized three of us; they took them to the mountains; they tied them up in the mountains and killed them with machetes and knives. There they died. Then they asked me which ones were the guerrillas, and I didn't tell them, so they slashed me with the machete; they raped me; they threw me on the ground and slashed my head with the machete; my breasts, my entire hand. When dawn came I tried to get home. By then I could hardly walk. I came across a girl from our village and she was carrying some water. She gave me some and took me to her house.

'The army also seized my 13-year-old brother Ramos and dragged him away and shot him in the foot and left him thrown on the ground. My brother and my parents and my other brothers and sisters had been in the house. The soldiers said, "They are guerrillas, and they must be killed". My brother saw how they killed my parents, my mother, my brothers and sisters and my little one-year-old brother; the soldiers machine-gunned them to death when they arrived in the village. Only my brother, Ramos, and I are alive. Our friends are giving us injections and medicines. We can't go to the hospital. I think they would kill us there.'

This account by a 17-year-old Indian girl from the tiny village of Chirren-quiché, near Cobán, describes a very typical counter-insurgency operation in a rural area of Guatemala. Such incidents are commonplace today; this individual occasion was in April 1982 and happened to coincide almost to the day with the first confrontation between troops of the Argentine military junta and British Marines on the island of South Georgia (see the earlier book by the same author, also published by Octopus, *The World's Elite Forces*).

Tens, if not hundreds of thousands, of largely innocent Guatemalan citizens have been murdered, abducted or tortured by a variety of internal security troops since the mid-1960s. The organizations collectively form a secret police and counter-insurgency force probably larger, proportionately, than that of any other country in the world. They include official security guards assigned as bodyguards to government functionaries; private security guards recruited from the police and the armed services for similar functions; and genuine 'death squads' composed of off-duty soldiers and policemen, and their targets are the obvious ones seen in earlier sections of this book — church leaders, lawyers, journalists, trades unionists and, of course, the Indian peasantry who, wittingly or unwittingly, provide succour for the large number of armed guerrilla groups which are extremely active and often trained by the PLO in Syria, South Yemen or, until recently, in the Lebanon.

The continuing state of virtual civil war in Guatemala started in the early 1960s during the regime of President Julio César Méndez Montenegro.

Guatemala is, and always has been, a largely agricultural country with a rigid population structure placing the whites of European descent at the top, the *mestizos* or half-castes in the middle, and the *indigenas*, or Indians of Mayan descent, firmly at the bottom. Slavery (called 'debt-bondage') was widespread in the country well into the 1930s, and only ended, somewhat strangely, under the military dictatorship of General George Ubico who established the foundations for the present totalitarian regime. Ubico was deposed in 1944 and a brief interregnum of a decade occurred during which a variety of attempts were made to turn Guatemala into a democracy. It was this period which saw the birth of a trades union movement, an increasing sense of identity among the Indians, and the growth of communism. This caused concern in the United States and led to CIA and State Department backing for the military coup of 1954 which put Colonel Castillo Armas in power. The Colonel was assassinated three years later, but his successor, Miguel Ydigoras Fuentes, continued his policies.

These policies of repression seemed bad enough at the time but were nothing compared to those introduced by Colonel Enrique Peralta Azurdia, who overthrew Castillo in 1963. Peralta started by suspending the constitution and followed through by founding the *Policía Judicial*, a special security force with powers to detain 'suspects' without warrant and hold them incommunicado for an indefinite length of time. As with the Nazi Gestapo, this force was rapidly filled with petty criminals and thugs, largely of low intelligence and extreme brutality. 'Disappearances' began to accumulate, as sociologist Gabriel Aguilera Peralta (no relation to the President) related in a study published in 1977. 'First people disappeared for a few days, and then they appeared again although they had been beaten. Later, things passed to the second stage; they disappeared for a much longer time and had been very severely tortured. And the third phase consisted of definite disappearance of the person, after beatings and torture. . . .'

For a brief period, it seemed as though the situation might improve. Although, in March 1966, the left-wing *Partido Guatemalteco de Trabajo* had been declared illegal and 28 of its members abducted, never to be seen again, the relatively progressive *Partido Revolucionario* came to power the same month led by Julio César Méndez Montenegro, one of whose avowed objectives was to come to terms with the various guerrilla groups. However, he was unsuccessful and became in retaliation even more repressive than his predecessors. Two new secret police forces were created: the *Policía Militar Ambulante* (PMA, or Mobile Military Police) and the *Guardia de Hacienda* (Border Guard), whose tasks were the suppression of guerrilla groups in the rural and border areas.

As in other Latin American countries, a secret organization of right-wing civilians and off-duty soldiers also came into being, known as the *Mano*

Blanca or 'White Hand', which is reputed to have been aided by the notorious Ku Klux Klan. This group of violent racists had as its stated objective the eradication of 'national renegades as traitors to the country', but was only the first of no fewer than 20 similar organizations formed during the first year of Méndez' rule, the second most feared of which was the *Movimiento de Liberación Nacional*.

Ultimately the 'death squads' from these groups became the real 'secret police' in Guatemala, and the government seemed to lose almost all control over their activities — certainly President Méndez did. That he tried to curb their activities is seen in his dismissal of his Defence Minister, Colonel Arriage Bosque, and Colonel Carlos Arana Osorio, to virtual exile abroad after the kidnap in broad daylight of Guatemala City's Archbishop: both men are known to have been active in the *Mano Blanca*. However, Méndez' power base was the military and they did not take kindly to this treatment of their colleagues. Colonel Arana, who had been in charge of the largely successful counter-guerrilla campaign in the Zacapa Province, returned to oust Méndez from power, and four years of 'official terrorism' ensued from 1970 to 1974. Hundreds of peasants and farm labourers simply disappeared, rounded up and exterminated by government-backed 'hit squads' who used methods originated by the German *Einsatzgruppen* in Poland and Russia for dealing with Jews and partisans. Some 15,000 people vanished from sight during this reign of terror before Arana was in turn replaced by General Kjell Laugerud.

For the first couple of years of Laugerud's presidency a semblance of normality returned to Guatemala, and the number of disappearances and obvious political murders declined. However, the disastrous earthquake of 1976 enabled the government to clamp down again under the pretext of preventing looting and civil disturbance. One of the first victims was the director of administrative services for the slum area of Guatemala City, Rolando Andrade Peña, a member of the centre-left *Frente Unido de la Revolución*, who was gunned down in the street. The following month the FUR's leader, Manuel Colom Argueta — who had served as Mayor of Guatemala City under Arana — was wounded in a similar attack. He publicly accused Laugerud and the *Policía Regional* and a few days later was killed, again in broad daylight, in a 1930s-style gangster attack with a sub-machine-gun.

By the time Laugerud came to power, the Indians in the rural provinces were beginning to get reorganized following their decimation during the Arana regime, and formed the new Guerrilla Army of the Poor which began carrying out effective raids on the homes of wealthy white landowners and on police and military garrisons and vehicles. Laugerud responded by initiating full-scale military operations and reprisals against civilians suspected of aiding and abetting the guerrillas, but eased up security measures in the cities during the run-up to the 1978 elections. This freedom — which actually included the right to hold political rallies in public — was short-lived. Laugerud was replaced by General Romeo Lucas Garcia who quickly formed the *Ejército Secreto Anti-Comunista* referred to at the beginning of this section.

One of the first actions of the ESA was to publish a list of names of people who had been 'tried' and sentenced to death. The first person on this list to die was student-leader Oliviero Castañeda. Along with thousands of other Guatemalans, Castañeda was out on the street for the annual celebration to mark the 1944 coup which deposed General Ubico. The roads were crowded with people, including large numbers of uniformed police who were present to keep the situation under control. A hit squad from the ESA, heavily armed, moved in on Castañeda from five unmarked cars and gunned him down in front of hundreds of witnesses. The police — presumably forewarned — did nothing. There was no attempt at pursuit and the culprits still remain free.

Trades union officials were next. Pedro Quevedo y Quevedo, secretary general of the union at the large Coca Cola bottling plant in Guatemala City, was murdered, and his successor finally sought asylum in the Venezuelan Embassy after three attempts on his own life. Manuel López Balan replaced him but was stabbed to death only a few days later. However, even worse was to come. In June 1980 almost every member of the trades union congress, the CNT, was arrested as they met to make the funeral arrangements for yet another executed union member. Armed police closed off the streets around the building where they were meeting and some 60 plain-clothed men of the security forces stormed into the building. The 25 congress members were hustled into police vans and driven away. None has since been seen alive, although unconfirmed reports claim that some of their bodies have been found in secret graveyards.

The government changed again in 1982, General Efraín Ríos Montt assuming the presidency. To begin with Montt paid lip service to civil liberties, and the overt activities of the ESA in the city streets declined. However, official terrorism in the country districts continued and life for the average peasant was still no different to what it had been a quarter of a century earlier — short, brutish and nasty.

Central control of the security forces — presumably paramilitary as well as official — comes from the *Centro Regional de Telecomunicaciones* in the compound behind the presidential palace. No doubt telecommunications form part of the work of the anonymous men who have access to this compound, but it is also known to be the base of the sinisterly named *Centro de Servicios Especiales de la Presidencia*, or presidential special service. This centre coordinated continued surveillance, abduction, torture and murder of suspected anti-government activists.

Eighteen months after he was elected president, Montt was deposed in a military coup (August 1983), but the country's new leader, General Oscar Humberto Mejía Victores, is no improvement. In response to complaints from international rights organizations, he gives the same excuses that all his predecessors have done — that the kidnappings and murders are the work of extremist right- or left-wing groups over which the government has no control.

Even though Mejía has repealed Montt's decree of July 1982, which established military tribunals empowered to try and execute political offenders without proper legal proceedings, this is just window dressing. In January 1984, for example, trades union official Amancio Samuel Villatoro was abducted. He was seen by another prisoner who later managed to escape and now lives in exile, Alvaro René Sosa Ramos. At the time they were both housed in a government interrogation and torture centre. After his own escape to a neutral embassy, where he was treated for the effects of electrical torture and gunshot wounds received during his dash to freedom, Sosa reported having seen a third trades unionist in the same centre, Silvio Matricardi Sala, whose mutilated body was discovered three months later near Escuintla. Persecution of union members and officials continues to this day, despite all the attempts of the United Nations.

Other Latin American countries
Although on a reduced scale compared with secret police activities in the countries so far mentioned, abduction, torture and murder are also tools of the trade for several other Central and South American governments, especially those of Guyana, Haiti, Honduras, Mexico, Nicaragua, Paraguay, Peru and Uruguay.

In Guyana there have been recent reports of police brutality, including beatings and the use of car batteries to administer electric shocks. However, this treatment has been meted out to criminals rather than political offenders, and Guyana does not possess a secret police force as such.

In Haiti, where President Jean-Claude Duvalier held power from 1971 to 1986, there was no political freedom whatsoever and the government's wishes were willingly carried out by the *Service détectif* (SD) or, more commonly, by the *Volontaires de la sécurité nationale* – the rightly feared *tontons macoutes*. The latter had an unusual tool which helped them terrorize the population, for they professed to be Voodoo adepts and could call on the supernatural to extort confessions! This, although it sounds far-fetched to Western minds, was a valuable weapon against the superstititious and poorly educated peasantry of the island.

The centre for secret police activity, including interrogations under torture, was the *Casernes Dessalines*, or military barracks, in Port-au-Prince. Many hundreds of alleged political offenders have passed through the

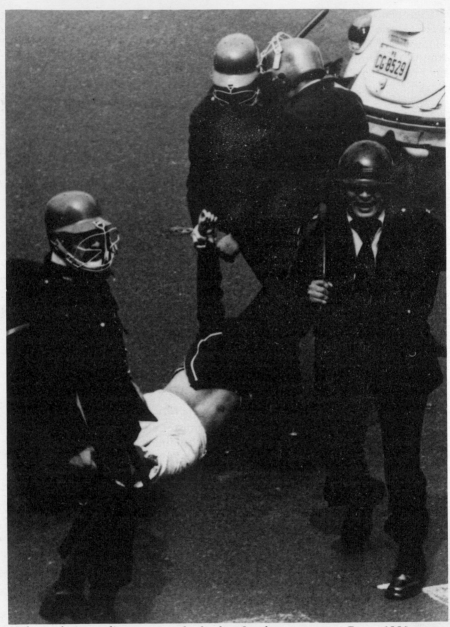

Helmeted riot police remove the body of a demonstrator, Peru, 1980.

barracks and into indefinite imprisonment over the years. Dozens are known to have been severely ill-treated and to have ended up in hospital or been killed. However, in March 1984, Duvalier issued an instruction to both his Minister of Justice and the Chief of Staff of the Haitian armed forces instructing them to 'strictly prohibit members of the Armed Forces from attacking the physical or moral integrity of any individual', particularly using torture in any of its forms, and demanding that no prisoner be detained for longer than 48 hours before being brought before a judge. As a result, arrests have declined and most detentions became short-term, but there are still many missing persons from earlier years whose fate remains unknown.

In February 1986 'Baby Doc' Duvalier was forced to flee into exile and there were widespread media reports that known members of the *tonton macoutes* were being slaughtered in the streets by the long-repressed population. At the time of writing, the overall situation remained unclear, but it can only be hoped that some form of democracy will now emerge in Haiti.

In Honduras, where the security forces frequently collaborate with those of neighbouring El Salvador in returning refugees, there are still isolated reports of people being detained without trial and being tortured, despite the election of President Roberto Suazo Córdova as the head of the country's first civilian government in 1982 and his expulsion into exile of the former head of the armed forces, General Alvarez Martínez. However, an almost bewildering variety of secret police organizations still exists, including the *Departamento Nacional de Investigaciones* (DNI), the *Cobras*, a plain-clothes intelligence group, the *Cuerpo Anti-Subsersivo* or anti-subversion corps, the *Fuerzas de Seguridad Pública* (FUSEP) or public security forces, and the military counter-insurgency unit TESON (*Tropas Especiales para Selva y Nocturnas*), a unit specially trained in jungle and night warfare tactics by the CIA.

Recent victims of these security forces include the leader of the Honduran electricity workers' union, Rolando Vindel González, who was arrested in March 1984 during a wage dispute. Public protests at his disappearance led to the army being called in to take over power plants. Although several other workers were arrested, they were all released in a short while. Vindel's whereabouts, however, are still unknown. Two other men, both accused of involvement with armed insurgents, were arrested during the summer of the same year and brought to trial. One of them, Osiris Villalobos, complained to the court that the FUSEP troops detaining him had used torture in order to try to extract a confession, but, when he tried to make a statement to journalists outside the courtroom, a DNI agent clamped a hand over his mouth and he was hustled away in a car. Neither he nor his companion have been seen since.

In Mexico, frequent complaints have been made about brutality and torture against the *División de Investigaciones para la Prevención de la Delincuencia* (DIPD) which is known to have abducted political and trades union activists. Many reports have appeared in Mexican newspapers following the eventual release of some prisoners, accusing the DIPD of various forms of torture, including beating with cupped hands over the ears, forcing carbonated drinks up the nose, the application of lighted cigarettes to the skin, beatings, and the use of electrodes on the most sensitive parts of the body. As in several other Latin American countries, a paramilitary undercover organization also exists, here known as the *Brigada Blanca*. Most of this group's activities seem to be concentrated in the rural areas and to be directed against the Indian peasants, some 500 of whom are known to have 'disappeared' over the last decade. Although the government officially denies any complicity in the activities of the *Brigada Blanca*, it cannot hide the presence of a secret detention centre known as *Campo Militar No 1* used by members of the group just outside Mexico City.

In January 1984 Amnesty International complained to the Mexican government about the murder by security forces of seven Indians who were members of a tribal movement campaigning for communal land sharing. In April two more people were killed and 30 wounded in shooting incidents and in May an 11-year-old boy was killed when plain-clothes gunmen, accompanied by uniformed troops, opened fire in the village of Techimal when its population refused to give them the names of leaders in another independent movement seeking communal land ownership. Other known or suspected members of similar groups have been abducted, and further reports of beatings and torture are still received regularly.

In Nicaragua, both the state security service, the *Dirección General de Seguridad del Estado* (DGSE), and the armed guerrillas of the *Fuerza Democrática Nicaragüense*, who continue to fight a military campaign seeking to overthrow the government, are known to use kidnapping and torture as terror weapons. The guerrillas mainly operate out of secret camps inside Honduras and are known to have American military and financial backing. Both sides in the struggle regularly abduct people believed to be collaborating with the other, and the FDN base their tactics on the official CIA manual *Psychological Operations in Guerrilla Warfare*.

In Paraguay, an official 'state of siege' has existed for the last 30 years, the protagonists being the right-wing totalitarian government of President Stroessner and the 'Chinese' wing of the outlawed Paraguayan Communist Party. Many people are known to have been in jail for the last 20 years or more, and reports from released prisoners who manage to make their way abroad claim widespread use of torture by the *División Técnica de Represión del Comunismo*, a department of the *Departamento de Investigaciones de la Policía* (DIPC). Methods used by the DIPC include the use of electric cattle prods and holding the victim's head in a tank of water, often polluted

Haiti — human skulls found in mass graves for unclaimed bodies.

with excrement. Beatings, confinement in tiny cells permitting no movement, *murciélago* — suspension by the ankles — and *secadera*, in which a prisoner is wrapped in a plastic sheet and sealed in a metal container, are other forms of torture used. Journalists and members of Christian aid organizations have also reported ill-treatment at the hands of the police.

A similar situation prevails in Peru, where power is wielded by the two political security branches of the police, the *Seguridad del Estado* and the *División Contra el Terrorismo*. Their main targets are Indian rights organizations in the rural areas, and testimonies of survivors from interrogation include descriptions of people being hooded and blindfolded, kept without food or water for several days, being stripped and beaten with sandbags, and being handcuffed behind the back then suspended from a pulley, sometimes with wet rags placed over the face to obstruct breathing.

Among those so treated was 26-year-old Juana Lidia Argumedo, who was arrested when she complained to the authorities about the murder by army forces of eight journalists in the village of Uchuraccay in 1983. She was detained incommunicado at a naval barracks near the village for a week before a civilian judge heard of her complaint and demanded her release. She later testified in court that, in the presence of a navy doctor, she had been severely beaten, suspended by her wrists and nearly suffocated, given electric shocks and raped repeatedly by marines. The court ordered a physical examination which confirmed her story, and she spent a period in hospital in order to recover, before moving to Lima to get away from anonymous death threats.

In Uruguay, many members of the *Movimiento de Liberación Nacional* have been detained and interrogated under torture in the country's top security prison, the *Penal de Libertad*, by the secret police, the *Organismo Coordinador de Actividades Anti-Subversivas*. Reports of torture before conviction in order to try to produce fabricated confessions are rife, the methods employed being identical to those used in Paraguay and elsewhere.

Other countries where long-term detentions of political opponents and the use of 'milder' forms of torture are also known to continue include Costa Rica, Cuba, Dominica, Grenada, Suriname and Venezuela, but it would be repetitive to go into detail.

CHAPTER FOUR

WESTERN EUROPE

FRANCE · GREAT BRITAIN · ITALY · SPAIN

In Western Europe, by and large, secret police forces are not needed to control home populations, and exist principally to counteract terrorism. The two principal exceptions are Great Britain, which has the Irish problem to contend with, and Spain, where Basque separatists have been using terrorist methods for many years in an attempt to establish a separate state. However, in all four countries listed, security forces do keep regular surveillance on extreme political activists and there are occasional public outcries when it is discovered that someone's telephone has been tapped or a prisoner complains that he has been beaten up while in police detention. I do not believe, though, that many people in Western Europe — now that Franco and the Greek Colonels have gone — feel that they live in police states, and most people are more concerned about traffic wardens or motorway police than about any form of 'big brother' organization watching them.

France

When General Charles de Gaulle entered Paris at the head of the Free French forces in August 1944 he was one of the most popular figures in the country; by the time he retired in 1969 he was one of the most hated and had already survived several assassination attempts. In the immediate post-war period his main problem was the communists, who had played a leading role in the *maquis* fighting against the Germans and who, understandably,

Student riots in Paris, 1968.

expected to play a similar part in the peacetime government. This was not at all what de Gaulle wanted and he used all the powers of the *Service de Documentation Extérieure et de Contre-Espionnage* (SDECE) to monitor communist activities and keep their leadership under surveillance. In the end the communists were excluded from the government, but a new problem was shortly to arise, that of Algeria.

Algeria had been colonized by France in the first half of the 19th century and was regarded by most Frenchmen — especially the white inhabitants of Algeria — as part of France itself. However, Arab nationalism was never far from the surface. In 1945 Arabs killed 103 Europeans: French reprisals rivalled those of the Nazis. Forty villages were bombed by French aircraft, and thousands of innocent people lost their lives (the total has never been established but could have been as high as 45,000). Thus, hundreds of Algerian Arabs who had served in the Free French forces under de Gaulle returned home when they were demobilized to find their houses gone, and their wives and families massacred. Is it any wonder that simmering resentment of French occupation turned to burning hatred and a desire to throw off the Gaullist yoke? Thus was born the *Front de Libération Nationale* (FLN), an Arab army led by competent French-trained soldiers but which also included terrorists of the most extreme views, including some former members of Hitler's own SS Arab Legion.

FLN policy was standard for any terrorist movement. It aimed through its acts of violence against Europeans to provoke the authorities into reprisals which would be so extreme as to drive moderate Arabs into the FLN camp. Atrocities on a vast scale were committed by both sides in the conflict, and for the first time since 1789 — when torture had been legally abolished in France — the French Army was given legal powers to use torture in the interrogation of suspects.

For a brief period during the worst of the atrocities de Gaulle was out of power, having been defeated over his Tunisian policies. Ever deceitful, de Gaulle allowed himself to be swept back into power on a platform of keeping Algeria French. This was a sham, because he really believed that the Algerian bloodbath would destroy the French Army and wanted to pull out as quickly as possible. Before he could do that, however, he had to consolidate his own position, which he did by forcing through a new constitution for the Fifth Republic which made the President, in effect, a dictator, and then getting himself elected President. Within months he was in secret negotiations with the FLN and in 1961 held a referendum on Algerian independence which received a resounding 'yes' from the millions of people sick of the bloodshed.

This betrayal of the people who had brought him back to power, particularly of the Army, led to a violent backlash. In Algiers, the Army, including the crack 1er REP — 1st Parachute Regiment of the Foreign Legion —

mutinied. Their opposition was short-lived and the regiment was disbanded, so the anti-Gaullists went into hiding, forming the *Organisation de l'Armée Secrète* (OAS, or Secret Army Organization). After Algeria finally received independence in 1962, they transferred their operations to Metropolitan France, engaging in terrorist acts against known Gaullist sympathizers who had helped in the Algerian betrayal, and nearly succeeding on two occasions in killing the General himself. Their activities allowed de Gaulle to maintain the special powers he had given the military and security forces in Algeria, and during the 1960s torture was routinely used by the SDECE and the riot police (the CRS) in extracting information from people — many of them innocent.

I was in Paris during the bitterly cold spring of 1968, at the height of the student revolt there. I can remember the lines of helmeted and shielded CRS advancing across a square against a crowd of demonstrators. As a tourist, I felt safe, and was even taking some photographs as the tear gas grenades started to go off. A CRS man shouted something at me (my French is schoolboy best) and I said that I was English. He swung his baton threateningly and demanded 'Camera!' I could understand *that* and handed it to him, but he didn't merely remove the film, he threw it to the ground and stamped on it. '*Allez!*', he shouted and, I confess, I ran. I have never been so frightened in my life, and I can share to a tiny degree, therefore, the feelings and apprehensions of those who have to live under such conditions every day of their lives.

Since de Gaulle's resignation and death, things have quietened down; the OAS terror has passed and normal civil liberties have been restored, although conscientious objectors to compulsory military service (which lasts 12 months) or its alternative civilian service (24 months) may still be imprisoned.

Great Britain

Apart from the intelligence services — MI5, MI6, the SIS (Secret Intelligence Service) and the Int Corps — the closest Great Britain possesses to a secret police force is the Special Branch. First formed in 1883 as a plain-clothes undercover unit to help combat bomb attacks in the UK by Irish Fenian extremists, it still has the same principal function, although its duties today embrace counter-terrorism in all its manifestations as well as surveillance of political activists who advocate violence. The latter include extremists of the Welsh and Scottish nationalist movements, and those who spread propaganda supporting the Provisional wing of the Irish Republican Army (PIRA) or the more recent Irish National Liberation Army (INLA), including distributing leaflets designed to undermine the morale of British troops serving in Northern Ireland. Other targets for Special Branch surveillance include members of the communist party, the National Front and

Mr Colin Hewett, one time overseer of special branch.

trades union officials.

Ireland has been a problem to successive British governments since the 17th century and, since 1969 when the present 'troubles' began, it has been IRA policy to create a mood in which the average Briton will say 'let them get on with it' — a policy identical with that of the FLN in Algeria, although a similar scale of violence has fortunately never been reached. It has been bad enough, however.

In 1968 the Civil Rights Movement in Northern Ireland, which was seeking equal rights for Roman Catholics in the Province, inadvertently brought about fighting in the streets of Belfast and elsewhere against Protestants, particularly Protestant extremists of the Orange Order. The level of civil disturbance led to the British Army being called in to maintain order, and since then the Army has worked hand in hand with the Special Branch in tracking down and arresting terrorists (of both sides), in seizing arms caches, and in generally trying to keep the level of violence down so that a political solution could, hopefully, one day, be worked out. The Dublin Agreement may produce that: only time will tell.

Special Branch officers are all highly trained professionals, usually recruited from the uniformed branch after a stiff entrance examination designed to test general knowledge and political awareness. After selection they undergo specialist training in the SB during their first year's probationary membership. This training includes detailed study of terrorist aims and methods worldwide, clandestine surveillance techniques such as telephone and car bugging, the use of long-range microphones, laser detectors (which can pick up a conversation inside a sealed room from the minute vibrations in the glass in the windows), and many other gadgets not available to the general public. Many of these have undoubtedly been developed for military purposes, primarily by the intelligence services and such organizations as the Special Air Service Regiment (SAS) — which also acts 'undercover' in Northern Ireland.

Military techniques often spill over into the police bailiwick in situations such as that prevailing in Northern Ireland during the 1970s (and, to a lesser extent, today), but it would be a mistake to believe that Special Branch learned all its methods from the SAS – it has been in existence far longer and has had time to assimilate the most effective techniques.

When the United Kingdom was hauled before the European Commission of Human Rights in 1976 and found guilty of the use of torture in Northern Ireland, it was one of the greatest legal travesties ever perpetrated — particularly in view of what was going on, and continues to go on elsewhere in the world, while this august body turns a blind eye. Fortunately, the ruling was thrown out two years later by the European Court of Human Rights, but the 'taint' lingers. What are the facts?

In August 1971 the British government reintroduced internment without

New Scotland Yard oversees the operations of special branch.

trial as permitted under the Special Powers Act of 1922, and several hundred people were arrested within days. Many were hooded and forced to spend long periods spreadeagled against walls. Some were assuredly beaten and kicked, or deprived of sleep, as revealed in the Compton Report which provoked another enquiry into interrogation methods leading to the Parker Report. This further report justified the methods used by the security forces, but a minority report produced by one member of the Parker Commission, Lord Gardiner, criticized them as 'procedures which were secret, illegal, not morally justifiable and alien to the traditions of . . . the greatest democracy in the world'. It was the minority report which the government accepted and similar interrogation methods were refused to the authorities for the future.

By the time that the government of Eire had complained to the European Commission, all such legally sanctioned acts had stopped, and the Maze internment camp was being closed and its 1,900 detainees released — much against the wishes of the majority of the British public. The prison itself remained, containing people convicted rather than just suspected of acts of terrorism. Some of the inmates then went through a period of 'blanket protest', refusing to wash and smearing their own cells with excrement, and accused the security authorities of subjecting them to this 'degrading treatment'. This time the European Commission rightly decided that the conditions were of the prisoners' own making. Faced with one failure, a number of IRA prisoners went on hunger strike, leading eventually to the deaths of ten of them — starting with Bobby Sands and ending with Michael Devine.

Special Branch has nothing to do with prison conditions or administration except in advising on security measures and, of course, interrogating prisoners. Its function is that of an investigative force, and although it is often parodied in popular fiction as being heavy-handed, it has done sterling work in containing most of the intended work of Irish activists within England — though not all, inevitably, and it is the terrorist 'successes' such as the Harrods' bomb disaster or the attack on the Tory party convention hotel in Brighton which produce the headlines. There would undoubtedly have been many more such tragedies were it not for the quiet, determined work of Britain's 'secret police'.

Special Branch consists of nearly 400 men organized into seven squads and led by a Deputy Assistant Commissioner — at the time of writing Colin Hewett — who reports through the Assistant Commissioner, Crime, to the Home Office (F4). About 70 officers at any given time are assigned to security duties at Heathrow and other airports and dockyards, where they can often be seen standing unobtrusively near immigration desks. A similar number are assigned to the protection of the Prime Minister, Cabinet Ministers and visiting heads of state. They work closely with the Security

Daily Mail

SATURDAY, MARCH 17, 1979

9p (CHANNEL ISLANDS 10p)

Conflict over Ulster brutality report

TORTURE: MASON IN NEW ROW

Daily Mail Reporter

THE controversy over whether there IS police torture of prisoners in Northern Ireland deepened yesterday, the very day an official report was supposed to clear it up.

In the Commons there were angry scenes when members discussed the Bennett Committee report into police treatment of prisoners in the province.

The report said that some prisoners had sustained injuries 'which were not self-inflicted'.

Many members inferred that the report was clearly indicating that the injuries had therefore been inflicted by members of the Royal Ulster Constabulary.

Northern Ireland Secretary Roy Mason did not directly disabuse them of this idea in the stormy questioning.

Conclusions

He accepted the report's 'broad conclusions,' he said, and was immediately implementing two of its main recommendations : that any terrorist suspect should have access to a solicitor at 48-hour intervals after being taken into custody, and that closed-circuit TV should be installed in all interrogation rooms

Mr Mason said also that

Blizzard baby dash

A PREMATURE baby, only a few hours old, was wrapped in cotton wool and tin foil to keep it alive last night.

Because of the ambulancemen's dispute, an Army ambulance had to carry the 2lb. 10oz. baby ten miles through blizzards to an intensive care unit.

Doctors were so worried that the freezing temperatures would kill the baby

Service (MI5) which has no powers of arrest, and with C13, the police anti-terrorist squad nicknamed the 'blue berets'.

There has been disquiet in recent times about the powers of Special Branch, particularly in the wake of the miners' strike, and many innocent people are concerned about what information on private individuals exists in Special Branch files — said to contain dossiers on some 1½ million people. Of particular concern is where some of this information may have come from. Normal police enquiries are the obvious and primary source, but it is widely believed that Special Branch has access to supposedly confidential computer records held by banks, credit companies, the Department of Social Security and the Inland Revenue as well as Customs and Excise, and the recent House of Commons select committee enquiry has done little to allay such suspicions.

Another cause of concern to many people is the arming of Special Branch and C13 officers with German-designed Heckler and Koch 9mm sub-machine-guns (which are actually manufactured clandestinely in the UK). These are the same weapons used by the SAS during the famous storming of the Iranian Embassy in London and are not considered by many experts to be suitable for security duties at crowded airports because of their lack of accuracy (a fault of all sub-machine-guns) and high penetrating power, which means innocent bystanders could easily be shot during an armed confrontation with terrorists. Certainly the sight of police patrolling in public with such weapons, although common in all other European countries, is not one which will be relished by the average Briton used to the unique tradition of an unarmed police force.

Of course, the police force has never been totally unarmed. Officers assigned to political protection duties routinely train using Smith and Wesson revolvers in shoulder holsters, and police marksmen armed with Parker Hale sniper rifles are used in situations where hostages are being held by armed criminals or terrorists. Tear gas, CS gas and 'stun' grenades are other weapons in the police arsenal.

Italy
In Italy, violence has been part and parcel of daily life for centuries. The Mafia is nothing new and the emergence of the Red Brigades in more recent years has added little to a confused situation other than to intensify the number of kidnappings — almost a national pastime — against which the plain-clothes police of the *carabinieri* labour, largely ineffectually. Half of the Italian problem is that those in power are usually involved with one or more of the criminal or terrorist groups, and historically many of those arrested by the police have had charges against them dropped because of pressure from above. Like France, in the immediate post-war period the biggest stumbling block against democratic government in Italy was the

Communist party which had been persecuted by Mussolini and which led the partisan movement fighting against the Germans in the mountains. Since the war, Italy has always been the Western European state most likely to become communist, and it is only the staunch Roman Catholic conservatism of the majority of the country's population which has prevented it turning into a second Yugoslavia. Nevertheless, the Communist party is strong and it was only by a narrow margin that Italy avoided joining the Communist bloc during the general European unrest and student revolt period of the mid-1960s to the mid-1970s. In this sort of climate revolutionary groups such as the Red Brigades were bound to flourish.

Italy has also been one of the prime targets for outside terrorism, particularly from Libya, because in European terms it is 'soft', with lax security and no firm policy against terrorism such as that adopted by Britain or West Germany. However, Italian security forces can be totally ruthless when they wish, and accusations of brutality and torture have been brought. In 1983, for example, four police officers were convicted of 'abusing their authority' during the interrogation of a Red Brigades terrorist. They were charged with having beaten him and tying him to a table, then forcing large quantities of water down his throat. The four were sentenced to periods of imprisonment varying from a year to 14 months, but a fifth man escaped punishment by getting himself elected to parliament and thus enjoying immunity.

In the early 1980s, torture was regularly used by the Italian security forces against captured members of the Red Brigades, particularly those connected with the kidnapping in 1982 of the NATO Chief of Staff, General James Lee Dozier. It is alleged that the police used lighted cigarettes and electrical shock treatment on some 30 people arrested in connection with this offence in order to extract information, although the government of the then Prime Minister, Giovanni Spadolini, denied the accusations.

Until 1984, the Italian political police had powers to detain suspects in custody for ten years eight months before they had to be convicted or released; this has now been reduced to six years but it is still a long time, and the criteria for those who may be so held are ambiguous. Some of those imprisoned under the preventive detention laws have resorted to hunger strikes, such as Giovanni Mulinaris who was arrested in 1982 but not charged with 'armed insurrection against the power of the state' until 1984. He required several months in hospital to recover before being released and put under house arrest.

Spain

One of the European countries with the worst record for human rights offences for decades under the Franco regime, Spain has been a democracy since 1978 when the current constitution came into effect, but the *Dirección*

General de Seguridad (DGS, or Security Directorate) still has wide powers, even under the revised anti-terrorist legislation of 26 December 1984 which replaces the earlier one of 1980.

The principal concern of the Spanish government is the *Euskadi Ta Askatasuna* (ETA, or Basque nationalist movement), which seeks through terrorist methods — including bombings and shootings in Spanish cities — to create an independent Basque state. Several thousand suspects have been arrested since 1980, although 'turnover' is rapid and most people are released fairly promptly, especially since the government introduced a *habeas corpus* law in December 1983 permitting the police to hold a suspect for a maximum of 72 hours before bringing a charge. However, under the anti-terrorist laws, the police can apply to detain someone for up to a further week while pursuing their enquiries. Six to seven hundred people a year are held under these regulations, and up to ten per cent complain about police brutality during interrogation. At the time of writing, some 80 cases of complaints against the police were under investigation by the authorities . . . but during 1984 only seven police officers were tried for brutality and torture.

CHAPTER FIVE

THE SOVIET UNION AND SATELLITE STATES

THE SOVIET UNION · CZECHOSLOVAKIA · EAST GERMANY · HUNGARY · POLAND · BULGARIA · ROMANIA

Although it is convenient to consider the secret police forces of Russia and her satellites together, there are vast differences between them — not in their operating methods, perhaps, but in other ways. In Russia, a secret police force vastly stronger than anything needed by the Tsars has existed continuously since 1917, and has been responsible for the murder of unknown millions of people — enemies of the revolution, ethnic groups such as the Ukrainians, Jews and, in more recent years, intellectual dissidents trying to bring reform by peaceful means.

In the satellite states — with the exception of East Germany where there is continuity from the Gestapo — secret police forces are a post-war phenomenon, and the peoples of these countries have not suffered the mass purges that characterized the Stalin era in particular. However, Poland, Hungary and Czechoslovakia have all been subject to invasions by the Red Army when their peoples tried to break away from Moscow's strings, and the KGB largely controls police policies within each satellite state.

The Soviet Union
Dzerzhinsky Square, Moscow — a name which probably conjures up more terror in the minds of more people than any other location in the world: the headquarters of the Russian Committee of State Security — the KGB — the largest, best organized and most greatly feared secret police force in the world. Behind the grey walls of what, in pre-Revolutionary days,

was an insurance society building, now exists the nerve centre of a multi-tentacled bureaucratic monster whose activities embrace espionage, counter-espionage, the running of the Gulag work camps, the security of the psychiatric hospitals to which dissident intellectuals are exiled, and the constant surveillance not just of the Russian people themselves but also of all foreign tourists visiting the Soviet Union. The KGB also provides intelligence officers at Soviet embassies abroad, 'minders' for Russian officials travelling overseas, security officers aboard Aeroflot airliners, at airports, dockyards and railway stations, and watchmen in all government departments of the Warsaw Pact satellite countries. It is, in effect, a state within a state and little of significance on either side of the 'Iron Curtain' escapes its notice. Even senior Soviet government officials, including Politburo members, live under covert but constant KGB surveillance. It provides funds, arms and training for many of the terrorist organizations abroad, regardless of whether they are communist in motivation or not, and frequently the recipients of KGB backing are not aware of the source. The KGB exists for two reasons: to prevent or contain dissent within the boundaries of the Soviet Union and its satellites, and to sow dissent everywhere else in the world that it can.

All this is well known by the average person. However, let us now examine how the KGB came into being and exactly how it does function in the 1980s. In order to do this we must go right back to 1917 and remember a statement of Robespierre's — from the French Revolution a century and a half earlier — of which Lenin was particularly fond. 'The attribute of popular government in revolution is at one and at the same time virtue and terror, virtue without which terror is fatal, terror without which virtue is impotent. The terror is nothing but justice, prompt, severe, inflexible; it is thus an emanation of virtue.' Marx and Lenin both seized upon terror as one of the principal tools of the new regime they hoped to forge, and unleashed against the people whose support they sought a weapon whose like the world had never seen before and hopes will never be seen again — although, as other chapters of this book show, there are plenty of people and governments anxious to emulate and, in some respects, surpass, the exploits and techniques of the KGB and its predecessors.

Prior to the Revolution, the Tsars of Russia had their own secret police force, the *Okhrana*. In Nicholas II's day it consisted of some 15,000 full-time spies and informers, but its powers and its results were negligible. Fewer than 20 people a year were executed — for political or criminal reasons — under the last of the Tsars. Lenin and Trotsky replaced the *Okhrana* with the ambiguously entitled 'All-Russian Extraordinary Commission' (*Cheka*), an organization headed by the fanatical Polish aristocrat, turned communist, Felix Dzerzhinksy, whose responsibilities included fighting counter-revolutionaries and preventing sabotage. Within three years the *Cheka* employed a quarter of a million people and executions of those accused of hindering or opposing the Revolution had grown to over a thousand a month. Within weeks of its formation the future shape of the Soviet secret services was firmly established. Russia was still at war with Germany at the time, it must be remembered, and there was an urgent need for trenches to be dug in the defence of Petrograd (formerly St Petersburg and today Leningrad). The *Cheka* energetically began rounding up 'bourgeois counter-revolutionaries' and herding them into work camps — the forerunners of the concentration camps — to dig these trenches. Moreover, the old Tsarist judicial system was replaced by 'revolutionary tribunals' which obeyed no laws, as such, in coming to judgement on those brought before them, merely relying on 'the circumstances of the case and *the dictates of the revolutionary conscience*'. This effectively gave the tribunals the power to convict anyone of the most trivial or even imaginary offence which could possibly be seen as against the interests of the revolution.

At the beginning of 1918 Lenin transferred the seat of government from Petrograd to Moscow and Felix Dzerzhinsky established his headquarters in what is now Dzerzhinsky Square, building within its walls a maximum security prison and interrogation centre — the notorious Lubyanka. To begin with, people seized by the *Cheka* were those who could be described in revolutionary terms as criminals, and included the work-shy, prostitutes and anyone found hoarding food supplies. Gradually, however, the emphasis changed and, instead of individuals, whole classes of people became victims of the *Cheka*. Dzerzhinsky's second-in-command, a Latvian, M. Y. Latsis, defined the organization's work as follows:

'The Extraordinary Commission is neither an investigating commission nor a tribunal. It is an organ of struggle, acting on the home front of a civil war. It does not judge the enemy: it strikes him . . . We are not carrying out war against individuals. We are exterminating the bourgeoisie as a class. We are not looking for evidence or witnesses to reveal deeds or words against the Soviet power. The first question we ask is — to what class does he belong, what are his origins, upbringing, education or profession? These questions define the fate of the accused.'

Until 1921, Lenin allowed 'fellow traveller' political parties to continue to exist, but after the sailors' mutiny at Kronstadt which began on the battleship *Petropavlosk* on 28 February and was ruthlessly crushed, he decided that all political opponents should either be jailed or exiled, thus giving the *Cheka* another target. The next stage, of course, would be to eliminate all opposition to his policies within the communist party itself. He had already, in 1919, established the People's Commissariat of State Control, whose task was surveillance of state officials and which was headed by Josef Stalin. He rapidly consolidated his own position, with Lenin's support (although this later declined), and by the time Lenin died in January 1924 Stalin was the single most powerful person in Soviet Russia.

Meanwhile, a new secret police organization had emerged alongside the *Cheka* which was eventually to take it over — the People's Commissariat of Internal Affairs, or NKVD. To begin with the NKVD was an administrative body to organize the work camps already run by the *Cheka* and to establish harsher camps in Siberia for enemies of the state. Head of the NKVD was G. G. Yagoda, a former pharmacist. To further confuse matters, there was a third secret police organization, the United State Political Organization, or OGPU, which set out to infiltrate the army. Its head was Viacheslav Menzhinsky. The OGPU also became responsible for the mass slaughter of peasant farmers who opposed Stalin's disastrous collectivization programme. Those who point to the 20 million Russians who died at German and Axis hands during the Second World War should remember the 20 million Russian peasants shot, strangled, bayoneted or sent to the labour camps during the 1930s by their own government. It was the most massive, the most outrageous, criminal act ever visited upon a nation by its rulers — yet in later years Stalin even boasted about it in public. Its full extent was not realized until after the Second World War, when records captured by the Germans were published for the first time. The peasantry retaliated by burning crops and killing livestock so that they should not fall into the hands of the commissars. The recriminations were felt everywhere. Stalin's second wife, Nadezdah, committed suicide after a violent row over his treatment of the peasants. Increasingly, he cocooned himself inside a web of secret police protection, creating a special personal bodyguard for his household from men of the OGPU.

The power of the OGPU grew in proportion. Soon it was not only running the labour camps, in which mortality was about ten per cent per year, but it was also providing slave labour to the tune of over a quarter of a million people a year for the public works programme of road-building and the like. Terror was still the OGPU's main weapon, as it is of the KGB. Innocent people on occasion are deliberately arrested precisely because they *are* innocent, thereby to sow terror in the hearts of friends and relatives who also know that the detainees are innocent.

The power struggle between the OGPU and the NKVD — which had between them completely absorbed the *Cheka* — came to a head during the 1930s. Stalin complained that his secret police had let him down by not implementing the collectivization programme and by failing to unmask conspiracy within the party ranks. Yagoda was one of the first to fall, but the purge of the secret police was soon extended to embrace the armed forces as well. One of the principal reasons Soviet military leadership was so poor at the beginning of the Second World War was that Stalin had some 30,000 of his ablest generals and field officers liquidated. Among those responsible, not just administratively but in actually pulling the trigger on occasion, were: Georgi Malenkov, Soviet premier from 1953–56; Nikita Kruschev, who ruled from 1956 to 1964; Alexei Kosygin; Leonid Brezhnev; and Yuri Andropov. Kruschev, who began the 'de-Stalinization' process, had the blood of hundreds, if not thousands, of Muscovites and Ukrainians on his hands. However, the man principally responsible was N. I. Yezhov, Yagoda's murderer, and known as 'the bloodthirsty dwarf' because he was less than five feet tall — but he in turn fell to the one man above all others whom the world recognizes as the creator of the KGB: Lavrenti Beria.

Beria was a Georgian, like Stalin himself, and both spoke Mingrelian as their native tongue; a common factor which brought them together. Both men were essentially coarse and enjoyed the copious amounts of vodka they drank well laced with pepper. Additionally, however, Beria was a womanizer, his tastes running particularly to young girls around the age of puberty, and he used his power as head of the NKVD to have girls literally dragged off the street and brought back to his flat. Born in 1899, he received a good education and joined the communists in 1917, rising through the *Cheka* to high rank in the OGPU during the civil war against the White Russians of 1919–22. During the late 1920s he was Yagoda's principal agent in Geneva and Paris, and in the 1930s was one of the prime movers in the campaign to recruit sympathizers in the west — among them Philby, Burgess and Maclean. After the Yezhov massacres, Beria was hailed virtually as a 'liberal', especially in his native Georgia, and in December 1938 he assumed total control of the NKVD with the title of People's Commissar for Internal Affairs.

The Yezhov pogrom left hardly anyone in Russia unaffected. Particularly singled out were foreign communists who had left their home countries either to escape from fascist regimes or through a desire to help in the 'great Soviet experiment'. These included over 800 Germans who had fled from Hitler — but they were not to have known that Stalin had a secret agreement with Hitler whereby not only did the German army practice manoeuvres in Russia but also the NKVD cooperated with the Gestapo in exchanging lists of wanted people.

Meanwhile, the labour camps were expanded. Most people are aware of conditions in these from the writings of Alexander Solzhenitsyn and others, but not everybody realizes that there were far more camps in Russia than were ever built by the Nazis. During 1936 to 1939 at least 4½ million people perished in the camps and, in particular, in the gold mines where men were forced to work a 16-hour day on pitiful rations and to sleep in tents even when the temperature was down to −51°C (−60°F): life expectancy averaged little more than a month under these conditions. Salvation for a few was to come from an unexpected quarter.

On 22 June 1941 German tanks started rolling across the border of divided Poland (which had been partitioned into German and Russian zones following the 1939 *blitzkrieg*), and Operation 'Barbarossa' — the invasion of the Soviet Union — was under way. During the first few weeks, the Russian armed forces suffered defeat after defeat, hundreds of thousands of men being encircled by the rapidly moving German forces and entering captivity. The Soviet military leadership, which had suffered badly during the Yezhov purges, lacked sufficient men of the calibre of the German generals and colonels to cope with the situation. Soon, Kiev had fallen, Leningrad was under siege and the Germans were into the suburbs of Moscow. It was only the recall of Marshal G.K. Zhukhov from Manchuria — where he had recently fought and won a campaign against the Japanese — and his appointment in charge of the defences of Moscow which saved the day; that, and the onset of the Russian winter for which the German troops were ill-prepared, since Hitler and his entourage had believed the campaign would be over long before.

However, in the intervening weeks Stalin, who had come under fierce attack for the lack of preparedness of the Soviet forces, managed to save his position when the activities of the German *Einsatzgruppen*, or extermination squads, became known. Advancing behind the main German front line, these squads of SS and police hunted down and ruthlessly murdered thousands of people. Stalin used this fact to turn the war into a great patriotic struggle for the salvation not just of the Soviet state, but of the Russian people themselves. Even those Russians who had originally welcomed the German attack, thinking it would free them from the communist yoke, now threw themselves into the defence. And volunteers from the Siberian labour camps (their chances of survival at the front were greater than in the camps) were organized into penal battalions.

The greatest irony of all in the context of the Second World War is that the NKVD continued to work clandestinely with the Gestapo, even though German soldiers killed NKVD commisars assigned to front-line army units (to preserve morale and report on subversive remarks), while Russian soldiers routinely tortured and executed anyone captured in SS uniform. The reason for this collaboration can be summed up in one expression — anti-Semitism — for the Soviet authorities were, and continue to be, as fanatical on this subject as were Himmler and his minions. This was to lead to a post-war tragedy which is still being acted out.

Two totalitarian regimes co-operating at one level while at war with each other on a second level is one thing. The co-operation given Stalin by Churchill and Roosevelt at Yalta is another. Both men detested the communist regime, and privately knew that confrontation with the Soviet Union was inevitable once Germany had been defeated. Both must have known about the Soviet labour camps and about the millions of pre-war executions. Yet, at Yalta, they agreed to repatriate all Russian citizens, willing or not, once the war was over. To the NKVD, any Russian soldier who allowed himself to be captured was a traitor, and so the world arrived at the cynical and tragic point where former Russian PoWs of the Germans were being herded back across the borders by British and American bayonets to face execution or the slower death of the labour camps.

This agreement was purely part of the carve-up of Europe which Churchill agreed with Stalin — omitting Roosevelt from some of the most critical negotiations. Churchill wanted to keep the Mediterranean an 'English pond' and was not interested in what happened in Bulgaria or Hungary so long as this goal was achieved. Thus millions of people fell under the Stalinist yoke in the satellite countries which now form the so-called Warsaw Pact. A disillusioned Roosevelt went into retirement to die, and the dynamic Harry Truman — who clandestinely even agreed to the re-arming of German PoWs prepared to fight on the Allied side against the Soviet Union — was unable to dispel the inertia faced with the wishes of Eisenhower, who wanted to retain Soviet cooperation until the Japanese had been defeated. So, Churchill rang down the 'iron curtain' (a phrase he originated in a speech on 5 March 1946) across Europe.

Within Russia a new curtain of blood was about to be created. Quite apart from returned prisoners of war, anyone — military or civilian — who had had contact with western civilization during the war became suspect, and the box-wagons to the Gulags began to refill. In August 1946 a witch-hunt of intellectuals also began; although diminished, it still continues today. Writers, musicians, film directors and philosophers came under the microscope first, and any who refused to toe the party line and rewrite their material in strict accordance with Stalinist doctrine soon found their privileges revoked and the spectre of a labour camp looming. Doctors and scientists were next, and cranks preaching pseudo-medicine and medieval genetics rose to the fore. Next, inevitably, were the Jews.

Stalin had always hated Jews quite as venomously as Hitler, and they had suffered appallingly in earlier purges. Now, in 1948, with the creation of the state of Israel and Golda Meir's first visit to Moscow to open the new country's first embassy there, Stalin went into an anti-Semitic frenzy. Cartoon characters sporting typically Jewish features began to appear and Jewish publications were prohibited. Many people went to the camps, including the wives of Molotov and Kuznetsov. Private homes were 'bugged' with electronic surveillance devices by the NKVD, as were foreign embassies: a radio-microphone was found in the house of the American Ambassador. Stalin even began to believe that his chief prosecutor, Beria, was a Jew!

Throughout the war, apart from strengthening the manpower of the NKVD in the army and increasing the number of forced labour camps, Beria had assumed a comparatively low profile, but after the war his powers increased in parallel with Stalin's paranoiac fantasies. In East Germany many former Gestapo and concentration camp personnel were 'whitewashed' and given new jobs in the *Sicherheitsdienst* — SD, or state security network — including, it is widely believed, the former Gestapo chief Müller, who was never brought to richly deserved trial for his war crimes. The SD, and the secret police of other satellite states, were creatures of an ever more powerful NKVD and, while enjoying a degree of regional autonomy, were subject to overall control from Dzerzhinsky Square.

In Russia itself a further half million people are known to have been executed or to have died in the labour camps between the end of the war and the death of Stalin in 1953. But, with the death of Stalin, Beria's own time had come. The official version of his death is that he was arrested after being denounced at a Politburo meeting in June, four months after Stalin's death, brought to trial and shot. Kruschev himself later told a different version to several people, including Harold Wilson in 1964. Beria, he said, was shot at the Politburo meeting by Marshal Koniev, who had managed to smuggle in a .22 calibre pistol through the MVD guards. (The NKVD had its name briefly changed to NKGB during the war and became simply the KGB following Beria's death. Precise meanings of the terms are unimportant because to all intents and purposes it remained, and remains, the same organization with the same duties.)

Following the deaths of Stalin and Beria, the Soviet government, now led by Kruschev, entered into a more liberal phase, and literally millions of people were declared innocent and released from the labour camps. But a new 'star' to head the KGB was in the ascendant: Yuri Andropov.

Andropov, who was to die shortly after attaining supreme power in the Soviet Union, had been born on 15 June 1914 at Nagutskaya, in the Caucasus Mountains, an area which, during the civil war from 1918 to 1920, was the scene of some of the bloodiest battles. In his youth he was a failure, lacking higher education, and became a river boatman — one of the lowest classes of Soviet society. In 1930, however, he joined the *Komsomol*, the communist youth movement which was directly comparable to the Hitler Youth in Germany. This was not surprising, since most Russian youngsters virtually had to join, but it was through this organization that 16-year-old Yuri Andropov was eventually to rise to power.

During the collectivization period and the later purges of the 1930s, Andropov wielded a butcher's axe and then started working for the NKVD while employed at the Rybinsk shipyard engaged on the expansion (by forced labour) of the Moscow-Volga canal. Precisely *what* he did for the secret police has not and probably never will be revealed, but in 1937 Andropov was promoted to the position of second secretary of the regional *Komsomol*. During the next year two of his party superiors were suddenly removed from office and the first secretary simply disappeared — presumably to the bottom of the Volga. Andropov's patron was Jacob Rappoport, then deputy leader of the labour camp programme. Under the latter's guidance, Andropov became first secretary of the Yaroslavl *Komsomol*. He then found an even more powerful sponsor, Nikolai Patolichev, a special appointee of the Central Committee of the Communist Party of the Soviet Union. And, after the 'Winter War' of 1939–40 between Finland and Russia which was a military stalemate and a diplomatic defeat for Russia, Andropov was — through Patolichev's influence with Stalin — appointed first secretary of the *Komsomol* in those parts of Karelia ceded to Russia as part of the peace settlement: not just a district now but an entire region. Here, he continued to work closely with senior NKVD officials, particularly in the deportation of thousands of Finns to Siberia to make room for families from other parts of Russia.

However, in June 1941 Hitler's invasion of the Soviet Union began and a week later Finland joined in on the German side. Within three months they had reoccupied nearly all of the territory lost during the Winter War. Andropov, living in the administrative quarters of a labour camp whose detainees were forced to build a new railway line from Murmansk in order to transport the supplies and weapons provided for the Soviet war effort by the British and Americans, became involved in helping to form NKVD extermination squads and partisan groups, although he never saw battle action himself. He was also one of those primarily responsible for organizing the labour parties of women and children who manually kept the vital Karelian timber flowing to Soviet factories — all the horses and cars or trucks in the province had been seized by the Red Army.

As the war drew to a close, however, Andropov's position began to seem less secure. One of those continual shifts in the power balance in the Kremlin which so characterize Soviet affairs left him without friends at court, so to speak. He was removed from his position as first secretary of the *Komsomol* and assigned a much more menial position as second secretary in the city of Petrozavodsk. He was lucky — many others lost their lives. Moreover, like Leonid Brezhnev and others, he was prepared to bide his time. He had not been implicated in the purges of the late 1930s, and when Stalin began to build up a new wall of confidants around himself after he dismissed the Politburo in 1946, Patolichev brought Andropov in with him, albeit as a fairly minor inspector in an unknown sub-department of the Central Committee.

In 1948 Patolichev's chief enemy in the Kremlin, Andrei Zhdanov, died, and there was an immediate purge of his accomplices, including Gennadi Kupriyanov, Andropov's immediate superior. (Unlike many, Kupriyanov survived, although he was badly beaten and tortured, and was later — under Kruschev — acquitted.) Three years later Andropov was admitted to Stalin's inner brotherhood but was to fall, with so many others, into disgrace after the latter's death in 1953. He was demoted and exiled to a position as a counsellor in the Soviet Embassy in Hungary, but within a year had been promoted to ambassador. He still held this position in October 1956 when crowds tore down the statue of Stalin in the centre of Budapest and began the Hungarian uprising, which was ruthlessly suppressed by the Red Army after Hungarian troops joined the protestors. Andropov emerged from this with the Kremlin credit due to a man who had helped suppress a revolution in a satellite state, and was reinstated on the Central Committee in 1957.

For the next few years Andropov steadily strengthened his own position under Kruschev, and after the latter's fall from grace as a result of the Cuban missile crisis in 1962, Andropov was elected to membership of the Central Committee Secretariat. Five years later he became Chairman of the KGB, on 19 May 1967; in 1973 he was finally admitted to the Politburo and in 1982, on the death of Mikhail Suslov, he became General Secretary of the Central Committee of the Communist Party of the Soviet Union. But it was as head of the KGB that Andropov achieved his greatest notoriety.

During the 15 years that Yuri Andropov was head of the KGB, the number of labour camps was increased to its present staggering 1,100, which accommodate some two million people. A similar number of people have to work in forced labour schemes while not being confined to camps. More ominously, Andropov exploited the idea of using psychiatric hospitals to house dissenters — after all, anyone who opposes the Soviet regime must be 'mad', so it makes a form of warped logic. Between his accession as head of the KGB and his rise to supreme leadership of the Soviet Union, the number of psychiatric hospitals in the USSR was expanded from 3 to 30.

The camps are administered directly by the MVD, or Ministry of Internal Affairs, but their inhabitants are consigned to them by the KGB and there are KGB officials present in each to determine policy and administer punishment or further interrogation if necessary, just as there is a KGB man somewhere in any Soviet organization.

Soviet prisons and labour camps do contain genuine criminals who richly deserve punishment, of course, but Soviet law can be interpreted so deviously by judges, if so instructed by the KGB, that in effect anyone can be interned on the flimsiest excuse. Doubtless the psychiatric hospitals also give asylum to the genuinely insane, but individuals and whole families who disagree with the regime are consigned to them for indefinite periods. There, they are given 'treatment' so bizarre and inhumane that the Soviet Union withdrew from the World Psychiatric Association in February 1983 in order to avoid being expelled, with consequent 'loss of face'.

The greatest and worst concentration of camps lies today in Mordovia — a region about 150 miles east of Moscow, which also houses the Vladimir

Andropov while he was head of the KGB.

prison in the city of that name. The camps are organized into four categories to cater for different degrees of 'crime': ordinary, reinforced, strict and special. Prisoners in special camps are housed in cells and have none of the minor privileges enjoyed by inmates of ordinary camps, such as visiting rights or food parcels.

Once sentenced to corrective labour, a prisoner will be driven there in a closed van called a *voronek* with two hard benches down each side. Especially 'dangerous' prisoners may be locked into one of two tiny booths inside the van, having to stand for a journey of up to 100 miles. If the journey to the designated camp is longer, prisoners are transported in special railway wagons known as 'Stolypin wagons'. Each of these contains ten compartments designed to hold eight to ten people, but as many as 30 are known to be forced inside on occasion for journeys which can last three or four days. There is one toilet in the wagon to which prisoners are taken individually by the MVD guards once or twice a day. Food and water are doled out grudgingly and in small portions — a piece of salt fish and a small loaf of bread a day, sometimes even less. In summer the lack of water causes acute discomfort to those in the metal wagons, which become ovens as the train wends its slow way across the steppes.

The following is part of one description of a typical journey. 'Fifteen people in a sleeping compartment. Everybody bathed in sweat. Food spoiled. For two days they did not take prisoners to the lavatory. People had to use the corridors . . . The windows were sealed shut. Only at the end of the deportation did they open the windows a little, but it did not help. People were lying naked on the floor. Dirt. Stink. Suffocation. One man died during the deportation. It was a terrible torture.'

Sometimes deportees are temporarily housed in transit prisons during their journey. Dark, crowded, filthy and crawling with insects, these are even worse than the corrective labour camps — or 'colonies' as they are euphemistically called today. A prisoner's first sight of the camp which will be his or her 'home' for the next few years is of the tall barbed-wire outer fence. Inside this is a high brick wall, topped with barbed wire. There are watch towers at each corner, manned by MVD guards with machine-guns and searchlights. Inside the walls are the barrack huts, each accommodating up to 200 people in crowded double bunk beds. In the special camps conditions are even worse, three to five prisoners being crowded into tiny cells with only a bucket for a toilet. The cells are usually damp, often with leaking roofs, and in winter the walls are rimed with frost while icicles dangle from the ceiling. Insects, mice and rats are other unsavoury problems. Prisoners in these special camps get only one hour's exercise each day, in a tiny yard about ten by seven yards in area.

In the ordinary barracks conditions are cramped and stuffy, suffocating in summer and inadequately heated in winter, and loudspeakers in each hut broadcasting propaganda and camp announcements — particularly executions — make sleep even more difficult. Prisoners are at least allowed to take a bath and do their laundry approximately once a week, but the quantities of soap provided are inadequate and wash-house conditions are usually filthy.

Hunger is a constant companion, not just in the special camps but even in the ordinary ones. Although the 'official' diet is supposed to give prisoners in the ordinary camps 2,500 calories a day, most people spend extended periods on reduced diets as punishment for minor offences, such as failing to get out of bed promptly at 6.00 am. The 'strict' diet is supposed to provide 1,700 calories, but reports of as low as 1,300 have been received — and these for people forced to do heavy manual labour every day. An account from one of the Mordovian camps says, 'Day after day we eat the same fodder: in the morning five days a week we get 55 grams of fish — rotten fish — and a bowl of watery gruel; at midday 21 grams of rotten *sboi* [offal] or lard, some watery, smelly soup or some borscht . . . in the evening smelly soup. We get damp bread with the thickness of a finger.'

One inmate of the Vladimir prison and other institutions, Vladimir Bukovsky, described his circumstances in the following words. 'I can't say that prison hunger was particularly agonizing — it wasn't a biting hunger but, rather, a prolonged process of chronic under-nourishment. You very quickly stopped feeling it badly and were left with a kind of gnawing pain, rather like a quietly throbbing toothache. You even lost awareness that it was hunger, and only after several months did you notice that it hurt to sit on a wooden bench, and, at night, no matter which way you turned, something hard seemed to be pressing into you or against you — you would get up several times in the night and shake the mattress, toss and turn from side to side, and still it hurt. Only then did you realize that your bones were sticking out. But by then you didn't care any longer. Nevertheless, you didn't get out of your bunk too quickly in the mornings, otherwise your head would spin.'

After a prisoner has served half of his or her sentence, he is legally entitled to receive up to three food parcels a year from relatives. However, the contents of these are rigorously restricted, and they may not, for instance, include any high protein or glucose products such as meat, sugar, honey or chocolate. The right to receive a food parcel is frequently withdrawn as a punishment.

Prisoners are also given a small cash allowance every month with which they can buy items from the camp shop, but these again are limited. They include jams, soups, cheese, bread, soap and tobacco, but nothing really nutritious since under-nourishment of prisoners is a deliberate policy and is intended to constitute part of their punishment. Despite all this, many prisoners are known to resort to hunger strikes in protest against camp conditions. Such action is, in fact, futile, since the rebels are simply beaten, put into solitary confinement and, after a suitable period of time, force-fed. Prisoners on hunger strike still have to work each day.

Medical treatment is virtually non-existent in the camps. Often there is not even a properly qualified doctor on the staff, just a male nurse or paramedic. Medicines are always in short supply and prisoners who ask to see the doctor are often accused of malingering and are punished. An estimated 25 per cent of all prisoners eventually contract tuberculosis, but stomach and bowel complaints induced by the inadequate diet and lack of vitamins are even more common. Even if a prisoner does manage to secure admission to a prison hospital, conditions are poor, and treatment usually has to take place in the corridors because of overcrowding in the wards. However, at least in hospital people receive better food, including milk, and admission to hospital is usually therefore reserved by the MVD guards for 'model' prisoners who are sent there as a reward either for good behaviour or for informing on other inmates. Deaths from lack of medical treatment are commonplace.

The type of work forced upon prisoners varies widely. Some work at timber felling, others in camp workshops making industrial components; some work in special factories and others are sent out daily in convict work gangs to help on construction sites. Quarrying and mining are the most arduous tasks, and are usually reserved for prisoners in the special camps. The normal expectation is for prisoners to work an eight-hour day, six days a week, but in practice their working day is often extended to 14 or 15 hours in order to adhere to production schedules. In the factories, where polishing and grinding operations are common, ventilation is poor and it is only recently that prisoners have been given respirators.

Another penalty of the labour camps which is particularly galling to those who oppose the regime on intellectual grounds is the political indoctrination talks. These go on for two hours every week and are supposed to be non-compulsory, but in practice anyone who fails to attend has a further black mark chalked up against him and may suffer punishment of varying degrees — he will certainly not get the early remission which is permitted under Soviet law but in fact very rarely applied. The level of the political lectures is almost universally low, the lecturers trotting out catch-phrases and clichés to which there are no proper responses.

Political indoctrination is accompanied by religious persecution, particularly of Jews, and there are regular hunts by the guards for religious literature of any description. One group of Jews in a camp in Perm during the 1970s stated that: 'The camp authorities inculcate nationalistic conflicts and incite other inmates against Jews. KGB Captains Maruzan and Ivkin stress in their conversation with non-Jewish inmates that all nationalities of the USSR must take a stand against Jews, particularly in the labour camps.

The administration provokes anti-Jewish incidents, utilizes informers and spies, and uses false witnesses in order to be able to impose additional punishment upon the Jews. Inmates who have had contact with Jews are summoned for discussions during which anti-Semitic sentiments are expressed, and they are told that protests against arbitrariness in camp rules are only profitable to the Zionists . . . The Jews are forbidden to observe their religious traditions . . . and forbidden to congregate even for a few minutes; such gatherings are immediately regarded as a Jewish assembly, a synagogue. Conversation in Hebrew or Yiddish is subject to punishment because these languages are not understood by the guards and therefore their content cannot be checked.'

Another Jew, Israel Zalmonson, was sentenced to eight years' imprisonment for conspiring to steal an aircraft in which to flee the country. He later said that 'more than once prisoners have told me that representatives of the administration and the KGB had warned them to keep away from the Jews, usually referring to them as "yids". They do this so as to isolate the Jews from the other political prisoners and create a ghetto atmosphere. Specifically Lieutenant Salakhov, the former head of my detachment, told the prisoner Yuri Dzyuba that "the Jews are our most bitter enemies" and for this reason he ought to keep away from them.'

Ladinsk prison camp.

Jews are not the only group singled out for special treatment in the camps. Tartars, Ukrainians and other ethnic groups looking for some form of self-determination within the state are also given special treatment. Particularly galling to a great many people is that Russian is the only language allowed to be spoken or written within the camps, and prisoners can be punished for speaking in their own language or even for being *sent* a letter written other than in Russian. There is, of course, total censorship in any case. Prisoners are generally allowed any number of letters inwards — although they are all read by the guards first — but they may only send out between one and three a month depending upon what type of regime they are labouring under.

One of the worst and most inhumane aspects of the Soviet labour camp system is that visits by friends and relatives are few and far between. Visits may be either 'long' or 'short'. A short visit lasts no more than four hours, a long visit up to three days in special family accommodation. However, even those in ordinary camps can have no more than six visits a year, while those on strict regime in prison receive no visitors at all. Pre-arranged visits are often cancelled, a further refinement of mental torture.

However, for political prisoners the guards and the strict regime are not the only hazards, for there is also a constant threat from the more violent criminal inmates. A Jewish would-be emigrant, Sender Levinson, described the following situation in his 'ordinary' camp. 'The enraged and embittered prisoners lived according to the rule of the jungle, with no compassion for the weak. The weak were raped and beaten. When I went down the mine at first I did not know that it was dangerous to walk down there alone. After about a week three men came up before me in a dark passage, pushed the torch out of my hand and tried to rape me. There are no women in the camp and weak men are therefore raped.' Later, Levinson was transferred to other camps. 'The guards', he reported, 'did whatever they felt like.

'The streams of blood spilled, the violence that I witnessed during that trip, both in the transit prisons and the trains, was incredible. In Odessa and Kharkov we were beaten with wooden hammers for our complaints about the lack of sanitary conditions and poor quality food. In Ruzaevka we were made to take showers with lukewarm water in a bath-house that had broken windows — in winter.'

Worse than the corrective labour in the camps and prisons in many respects is the brainwashing under drugs of political offenders in the psychiatric hospitals which were so drastically expanded by Andropov. Under both Soviet civil and criminal law, no individuals may be forcibly detained in a psychiatric institution against their will unless they are dangerous to themselves and others. Soviet authorities have used this ambiguous wording to interpret dissidence or the spreading of anti-Soviet propaganda as being 'dangerous', and hundreds of people have been incarcerated in mental hospitals since the early 1970s — many are still there.

In the case of political offenders, it is rare for even a pretence to be made that the person has been examined by a clinical psychologist. Moreover, trials are commonly held with the defendant either lacking legal counsel or even being absent. People are often seized on the street or summoned to a government office on some pretext where, to their surprise, they are suddenly faced with a psychiatrist. In the cases where such 'interviews' do take place, the psychiatrist will invariably be employed by the KGB or MVD and will have clear instructions what diagnosis to present to the court. As a rule, such examinations last a mere 10 to 15 minutes!

Known special psychiatric hospitals for the detention of 'especially dangerous' people can be found in Chernyakhovsk, Dnepropetrovsk, Leningrad, Oryol, Kazan, Sychyovka, Smolensk, Talgar, Tashkent, Blagoveshchensk and Rybinsk, and detainees usually serve a sentence of 15 to 20 years. They have no privileges or rights whatsoever, they cannot appeal to anyone, and they are permitted only rare visits by relatives under closely supervised conditions. 'Patients', especially Jews, are often humiliated, beaten or raped by drunken MVD guards. However, the worst aspect of the psychiatric prisons is the use of drugs to induce illness, confusion, disorientation and other effects in perfectly healthy people. Insulin, for example, administered to a non-diabetic, brings on a state of clinical shock. Neuroleptic drugs administered in large doses rather than the closely controlled amounts needed for genuine psychiatric help produce a form of artificial Parkinson's disease. Aminazin is another drug which brings on acute depression.

The purpose of administering these drugs is to persuade dissidents to relent and confess that their ideas were mistaken. Many people suffer from such treatment over periods of months or years. Leonid Plyushch, a computer expert from the Ukraine, was arrested in July 1973 and consigned to the special hospital in Dnepropetrovsk. When his wife managed to gain permission to visit him two months later she said, 'it was impossible to recognize him. His eyes were full of pain and misery, he spoke with difficulty and brokenly, frequently leaning on the back of the chair in search of support. His effort at self-control was evident as from time to time he closed his eyes, trying to carry on a conversation and to answer questions. But his inner strength was exhausted. Leonid Ivanovich began to gasp, to awkwardly unbutton his clothing . . . his face was convulsed and he got cramp in his hands and legs. Leonid Ivanovich could not control himself, and it was he who asked that the meeting be ended ten minutes ahead of time.'

Plyushch had been treated in massive doses with the tranquillizer haloperidol. Two months later his condition had further deteriorated and he told his wife to stop sending him technical books because he could no longer concentrate sufficiently to understand them. Later, in 1974, the 'doctors' changed his treatment and began administering insulin. His wife found

A view over the walls of Oryol special psychiatric hospital.

him unrecognizable, 'great dropsical swelling had occurred, he moved with difficulty and his eyes had lost their liveliness'.

Sulfazin is another drug sometimes used to try to make people 'confess'. This produces a raging fever, often accompanied by haemorrhoids. 'One of the patients called the doctors Gestapo. They prescribed injections of sulphur. This patient groaned loudly for 24 hours, mad with pain he tried to hide himself under the bed, in despair he broke the window and tried to cut his throat with glass. Then he was punished again, and repeatedly beaten up. He kept asking everyone, "Am I going to die?", and only when he really did begin to die and another patient noticed it did they stop the sulphur.'

Despite all this, domestic opposition to the Soviet system continues to grow. Why are people willing to put themselves at such risk? The Russian writer Yuri Krotkov, who defected to the West while on an Intourist package holiday to London, sums the position up as follows in his book *The Angry Exile* (Heinemann):

'This struggle of minds, of human ideals and aspirations, cannot be prevented; it knows no limits. Moreover, in its essence it does not depend on whether or not there is a thaw in the cold war. It is a mistake to think of this fight for intellectual and aesthetic freedom as an appendage of the cold war, to view this life-and death struggle in the Soviet Union as merely something to be exploited by Western ideologists and diplomats, to consider it just another weapon in the glamorous propaganda campaigns that now and again flare up, and then subside. The cold war is a game — a monstrous one, played in the shadow of an atomic holocaust, to be sure, but not without bluff on both sides. It is no different from so-called peaceful co-existence. But for me — and above all, for that handful of unhappy Soviet intellectuals who dare to challenge dictatorship over the human mind — this struggle is something very different, something more noble, something more fateful, something which — to use Pasternak's masterful expression — "smells of immortality".'

The satellite states
In Czechoslovakia today the main targets of the Ministry for State Security — apart from foreign spies, saboteurs and terrorists, of course — are those campaigning for the rights of the country's Magyar minority and members of various religious groups. One spokesman for the Magyar cause, Miklos Duray, was arrested in May 1984 for opposing a new law which would reduce the teaching of Hungarian in Czech schools. He has never been brought to trial and is still in prison in Bratislava. Other people, especially Roman Catholics, have been arrested for 'unauthorized' teaching of children in their homes. Compared with conditions in Russia the situation in Czechoslovakia is a great improvement though, and sentences against political or religious activists are mild. Many people, however, have to endure what is called 'protective surveillance' for a period of time after their release. This entails having to report to their local police station twice a day, having to get a special permit to travel outside the town where they live, and having to endure police raids of their homes at any time of the day or night.

In East Germany the Russians took over much of what was left of the Nazi Gestapo and *Sicherheitsdienst* networks in 1945, and large numbers of former SS officials who had — as mentioned earlier — been clandestinely cooperating with the KGB had their records 'whitewashed' and became leading figures in the post-war *Ministerium für Sicherheitsdienst* (MfS, or Ministry for State Security). Today, the main task of the MfS seems to be controlling the large numbers of Germans trying to emigrate to the West, the most obvious sign of the degree of disenchantment with the regime being the fact that the government had to build a wall across Berlin to keep its own people in. Just before you reach 'Checkpoint Charlie' in West Berlin, there is a poignant memorial to those East Germans who have been gunned down over the years while trying to escape over the wall.

Although the authorities have relaxed the laws against emigration in recent years, large numbers of people are refused permission for no stated reason, and if they persist may be arrested for 'obstruction'. That the MfS keeps close watch on those who have applied to emigrate is shown by the case of Ramona Philipp, the wife of an imprisoned conscientious objector to compulsory military service. She and five friends, who had also applied to emigrate in March 1984, met at a café in East Berlin whence they walked separately to the Permanent Commission of the West German government. Two of them were arrested the same day and the others shortly afterwards, and all were at the time of writing serving sentences of between 16 and 20 months' imprisonment.

What is most ironic, and most clearly demonstrates the communist's essential pragmatism, is that many hundreds of political prisoners in East Germany have been released to the West after the West German goverment 'ransomed' them in cash ('hard' Western currency being desperately short in East Germany). Over 2,000 people found freedom this way in 1984 alone.

Hungary has always been one of the satellite states whose population is generally most opposed covertly to membership of the Warsaw Pact, and it is significant that the Hungarian army is one of those in which the Soviet authorities place the least trust and which is accordingly kept very small. The repercussions of the 1956 revolt are still felt more keenly in Hungary than those of the 1968 low-key attempt in Czechoslovakia, and perhaps for this reason the KGB leash is fairly relaxed in public — to avoid provocation. Nevertheless, those who refuse to accept compulsory military service — other than, for some strange reason, Jehovah's Witnesses and Nazarenes — are sentenced to imprisonment. Special rules have been drawn up for the latter religious sects permitting them to serve without bearing arms, but the same rules do not apply to conscientious objectors of other sects.

Poland has, of course, been much in the public eye ever since the Solidarity movement came into prominence in 1980 and, quite apart from Red Army and KGB involvement, the powers of the KBW — the Ministry of Internal Affairs — have been increased. Beatings, torture and non-judicial imprisonments have increased, and many people have 'disappeared'. During the immediate Soviet reaction to the Solidarity trades union movement, at least 10,000 people are known to have been placed in internment camps without trial, although these camps are reported to have been disbanded at the end of 1982. Within this critical period, however, the KBW appear to have enjoyed free rein to beat, kick and batter with rubber truncheons anyone they chose. Police dogs are also reported to have been turned loose upon citizens who did not submit meekly to arrest.

In Poland today, private houses, business premises and factories are routinely subjected to searches by the KBW looking for evidence of Solidarity connections, despite the amnesty of 21 July 1984 which was designed to commemorate the 40th anniversary of the establishment of the Polish People's Republic. Although this amnesty does not expire until the end of 1986, and despite the fact that hundreds of Solidarity workers have either been released from confinement or had charges against them dropped, it is more than possible that it has been a ploy to give the government breathing space prior to a new clamp-down after the amnesty has expired.

In both Bulgaria and Romania (the other partners to the Warsaw Pact) there are similar curbs on what we in the West would consider normal civil liberties, including restrictions on emigration and prison penalties of up to five years for those who seek to do so. Would-be emigrés are often severely beaten up once imprisoned, as an example to others.

CHAPTER SIX

AFRICA

ANGOLA · CAMEROON · CHAD · CONGO · ETHIOPIA · GHANA · MOZAMBIQUE · NAMIBIA · RWANDA · SOUTH AFRICA · UGANDA · ZIMBABWE

For the purposes of this book, north African countries such as Libya have been grouped with the Middle East because their cultural, ethnic, religious and political relationships are closer than with the central and southern states of Africa. Most of the countries covered in this chapter have either suffered recent wars, are still at war, or are at least under some form of state of emergency due to guerrilla activity by political opponents of the present government. For this reason, secret police and other security and counter-insurgency forces are particularly strong and have wide powers to arrest and detain people without trial. Torture and political killings are rife, and in most places secret policemen are immune from legal prosecution. In those rare cases where the friends or relatives of a person who has been tortured or killed succeed in bringing officials to trial, the court verdict is almost always acquittal, no matter how strong the evidence in the prosecution's favour.

Most people in Europe or America, if asked to point a finger at a repressive or a racialist regime in Africa, will unhesitatingly name the Republic of South Africa without a further thought. What is usually forgotten is the deep-rooted tribal antagonism among many of the black peoples which is as racialist as any similar attitudes between people of different skin colour. In Uganda, for example, this has led to virtual genocide with literally hundreds of thousands of people being killed not just under Amin but also subsequently. Ethiopia is a similar case in point.

However, since South Africa is the country which concerns and interests most people, I have tried to explain the historical background to the present conflict, not in order to excuse apartheid but, hopefully, to show why it exists and how virtually impossible it is to persuade the white South Africans to abandon it, sanctions on trade and sport notwithstanding. Perhaps it would be better to re-open a normal dialogue and let free interchange of ideas exert a moderating influence? Certainly, passing decrees or resolutions in the United Nations, throwing one's hands up in horror, and erecting a form of wall around the country are never going to solve anything.

Angola
After a bitter civil war in which the present left-wing government came to power with the help of Cuban military forces, there is still a military confrontation in Angola in which the supposedly disbanded *Direcção de Informação e Segurança de Angola* (DISA, or Security Information Directorate) continues to play a clandestine part. All the officials serving with the secret police were arrested in 1979 in a great show of publicity, but all were released and the security forces are still working actively, in hand with the army, combating the South African-backed *União Nacional para a Independência Total de Angola* (UNITA). As in any guerrilla war, both sides are guilty of torture and murder of suspects without any pretence at normal legalities.

In April 1974 a coup d'état in Lisbon heralded the beginning of the end for 400 years of Portuguese rule in Angola, Mozambique and Guinea, and independence left the country in a state of utter turmoil with deep political and tribal antagonism between the communist People's Movement for the Liberation of Angola (MPLA) which holds power today, the Northern Angolan People's Union (FNLA) and UNITA, formed by Jonas Savimbi in 1966. Even prior to independence, these three organizations had been at each other's throats, and terrorism, ruthlessly crushed by military means by the Portuguese government, seemed to rule. The three groups were geographically distinct and, after the coup in Lisbon, became fratricidally locked in a long war for superiority. MPLA supporters began to be sent to the Soviet Union for military training in December 1974, and the first supporting Cuban troops arrived in April 1975. Although there was concern in the West, the United States had just withdrawn messily from the fiasco of Vietnam and was unwilling to lend a hand in another guerrilla war of attrition overseas. The South African government was more closely involved and concerned, for a communist base in Angola into which the SWAPO terrorists could retire with impunity from Namibia, was the last thing Prime Minister Botha or his supporters wanted. Strangely, several neighbouring African states normally bitterly opposed to the South African regime were equally fearful of a communist Angola, including the Ivory Coast, Zambia and Zaire, and South Africa agreed to lend military aid to the FNLA and UNITA providing they would put aside their differences and work together against the MPLA.

From being in a purely advisory situation, South Africa rapidly acquired the status of principal arms-supplier for the anti-communist forces and then moved into a full war state, although the number of South African troops involved never actually exceeded 2,000 or so. The American CIA and special forces were also involved, but on a very low-key basis. Meanwhile, Cuban troops kept pouring into Angola while support for the South African presence among neighbouring black governments declined, and in March 1976 the final South African Defence Force troops withdrew. However, they left the opposition UNITA forces well trained, supplied and motivated, and the struggle continues to this day.

In 1980, after the supposed disbandment of DISA the previous year, the Angolan government created a new Ministry of State Security and started work on a new high-security prison in the capital, Luanda. Since then, reports of illegal detention, torture, and execution without proper trial have continued to increase, and over 1,000 people are currently believed to be being held incommunicado.

Anyone who opposes the government is liable to be arrested without notice by the security police: for example, playwright Fernando Costa Andrade was arrested in 1982 for producing a satirical drama which mocked President Agostinho Neto and is still in custody. More recently, in 1984 over a hundred prisoners accused of both diamond smuggling and of working for the CIA were tried, and five sentenced to death, although two were later acquitted and three had their sentences deferred. Many people arrested at this time complained afterwards of security police brutality, the methods being painful but unsophisticated, usually involving beatings and electric shock treatment.

At least 31 death sentences have been passed against alleged UNITA guerrillas in the last couple of years on charges including treason, spying and sabotage, although only one — Isaias Jeremias Nangolo — is known to have been executed.

Cameroon

In April 1984, only three months after a presidential election had brought Paul Biya to power in Cameroon, army units based close to the capital of Yaoundé attempted a coup which was defeated by loyalist forces. Since that time the government is alleged to have executed some 120 people accused of complicity, although it only acknowledges less than half this number. The instrument of investigation in Cameroon is the *Brigades Mixtes Mobiles* (BMM), a paramilitary force responsible for interrogation whose methods frequently include humiliation, such as pouring urine and excrement over manacled prisoners, and torture, such as beatings and sexual harassment of women. A year after the attempted coup, one pregnant woman was tortured by being hung upside down from her ankles and whipped, as a result of which she suffered a miscarriage. The main centre for interrogation appears to be a room known as *la chapelle* (the chapel) in the BMM's Yaoundé headquarters. The government is also known to have various labour camps and 're-education centres' secretly established in the countryside.

Chad

Like Angola, Chad has been in a state of almost permanent civil war for the last few years, the government of President Hissène Habré being supported by French military forces, and that of the deposed President Goukouni Oueddeï by the Libyans, although both countries have now reduced their armed presence to a far lower level than in 1982–83.

President Habré was brought to power by the armed forces of Northern Chad in October 1982, and a wave of 'disappearances' and executions, not just of known opponents but also of those suspected of having sympathies with Oueddeï's regime, swept the country. Apart from the army, the principal organization responsible was the *Département de la Documentation et de la Sécurité* (DDS, or security police), whose headquarters are in the capital, N'Djamena. Apparently random attacks on villagers suspected of helping or harbouring Oueddeï guerrillas are also known to take place, sometimes in reprisal for atrocities against government troops which include mutilation and torture. For example, in September 1984 over 200 people in villages in the Moïssala district were either killed or abducted, and many others are known or believed to be still held in custody without benefit of legal trial.

Congo

The justification for a secret police force is usually counter-terrorism, although both expressions can have many different meanings. The Congo has its secret police force and its methods include torture and secret executions, but its main target is guerrillas from the neighbouring Central African Republic seeking to overthrow the government and whose own methods include the indiscriminate killing of innocent civilians, such as the ten people murdered when a bomb was exploded in a cinema in Brazzaville in 1982.

The secret police — the *Direction Générale de la Sécurité d'Etat* or DGSE — arrested 12 people suspected of complicity in this atrocity and, although most were subsequently released, three are believed to be still in detention behind the closely guarded walls of an estate on the outskirts of Brazzaville known as the *Cité des 17*, which is the DGSE interrogation centre. One of these men, Eugène Madimba, is alleged to have been tortured in order to extract the names of accomplices. Methods include beatings, electric shock treatment and handcuffing prisoners to door frames for periods of several hours. A Ugandan refugee suspected of espionage received similar treatment in 1982 before being released. Five other people are known to have been held in the *Cité des 17* on similar charges of causing explosions and one, Claude-Ernest Ndalla — an official of the Congolese Labour Party who had been arrested several times before the latest occasion in 1984 — has said that the DGSE used drugs to try to force information out of him.

A sign that President Denis Sassou Nguesso is beginning to adopt a less hard line against political offenders came in November 1984 with the release from prison of former President Joachim Yhombi–Opango, who had been held in detention without trial since he was deposed in 1979. Other prisoners have either been released as well, or their imminent release promised.

Ethiopia
Among all the somewhat self-congratulatory euphoria attending the genuine attempts of Bob Geldof and others to ease the famine in Ethiopia during 1984–85, one fact is frequently forgotten and is certainly not widely covered by the media-at-large — and that is that the poverty-stricken and under-nourished inhabitants of what is not one of the most hospitable countries in the world also have to survive under one of the most repressive and barbaric of political regimes.

Formerly known as Abyssinia, and incorporating the Italian colony of Eritrea, Ethiopia is a mountainous country with deep rift valleys draining into the Nile, and is for the most part normally a fertile area with plenty of natural grazing and a wide variety of wildlife. Its inhabitants are warlike and the country has had a history of invasions and counter-invasions going back centuries which, in modern terms, culminated in the Battle of Adowa in 1896 during which 6,000 Italian invaders were killed and a further 1,700 taken prisoner. The country as it is known today came into existence in 1930 when Ras Tafari, son of Ras Makonnen of Harar — one of the heroes of the battle — assumed the throne. European-educated, sophisticated and, by African standards, enlightened, Haile Selassie I, as he was known, ruled well, one of his first steps being to abolish slavery. He also inaugurated a constitution, a civil service and the beginnings of a proper educational system designed to help destroy the medieval feudalism which controlled most of the country.

In 1934 Mussolini exploited a minor incident to give him an excuse to invade Ethiopia, and the brave but inadequately armed tribesmen were beaten down by modern tanks, aircraft and the use of mustard gas in a campaign which, nevertheless, lasted three years. The British helped expel the invaders during the early years of World War Two and Ethiopia fell under British administration for a while until Haile Selassie managed to unite Eritrea as part of the country in 1947, introduced a new constitution in 1955, and held the first elections in 1957. An attempted military coup in 1960 was thwarted, but a subsequent one in 1974 was successful and, ever since, Ethiopia has been in a state of virtual civil war with dissident tribal groups from several regions seeking independence, notably the Oromo Liberation Front, the Tigray People's Liberation Front and the Ethiopian People's Democratic Movement, as well as members of various churches. The government's principal security and counter-insurgency agency, apart from the army, is the Central Revolutionary Investigation Department (CRID) whose headquarters are in the capital, Addis Ababa, and whose members are known colloquially as 'the third police'. The origin of this name is obscure, but the fact that they administer the 'third degree' in their efforts to extract information from prisoners may have something to do with it.

Literally thousands of people 'disappeared', were imprisoned, tortured, or otherwise maltreated during the so-called 'red terror' campaign of 1977–78 aimed against the various dissident groups, and at least 5,000 people are known to have been killed. The government used, and still uses, the most brutal and often primitive methods of 'persuasion' on suspects, pariticularly those believed to have been involved in armed insurrection. These methods include hanging prisoners from their wrists and ankles and beating them, especially on the soles of the feet which is particularly painful; raping women and tying heavy weights to the testicles of male prisoners; burning with boiling oil; electric shock treatment; and crushing hands and feet using crude blacksmith's tools. Since the people in general suffer from malnutrition and lack of general medical attention, some of the results may be better imagined than described, and death under interrogation is common.

One part of the community particularly singled out for persecution by the CRID was Beta Israel, the Ethiopian Jews otherwise known as *Falashas*. Imprisonment for the simple act of religious observance, or for attempting to seek a visa to emigrate to Israel, was commonplace before, in the midst of the famine, the Israeli government executed its remarkable secret evacuation scheme, airlifting thousands of Ethiopian Jews to safety in C-130 Hercules transport aircraft (similar to those used during the daring Entebbe raid) from isolated desert airstrips.

With the eyes of the world on Ethiopia, overt killings and kidnappings of suspected political, tribal and religious leaders have diminished, but it would be a mistake to think that they do not still occur under conditions of greater secrecy. The present government came to power in a bloodbath. In November 1974, immediately following the coup, it was announced that 60 prominent political prisoners had been shot by the army, including the former head of state, Brigadier Aman Andom, as well as members of Haile Selassie's family and other senior officials. (Andom was, in fact, killed during a gun battle, but the others were executed by firing squad.) At the time of writing ten members of Haile Selassie's family were known to be still held in detention more than ten years after the coup, including Tenagnework Haile Selassie and her four daughters.

Before the current famine, many people attempted to escape the regime by fleeing into the neighbouring tiny state of Jibuti. This turned out to be a mistake because the security forces of that French-speaking country (the *Brigade Spéciale de Recherche de la Gendarmerie* and the *Service de Documentation et de Sécurité*) frequently use torture even in the investigation of minor traffic offences, and collaborate with the Ethiopian army in forcibly returning refugees. During 1983–84, some 32,000 refugees were 'voluntarily' returned to their homeland, many of them to face torture or execution for anti-government activities.

Among those still in detention at the time of writing were 18 members of the Ethiopian People's Democratic Alliance accused of distributing subversive propaganda leaflets; a former Senator; an official of the Ethiopian Orthodox Church; Mengesha Gebre-Hiwot — the erstwhile Minister of Education; the Governor of the Agame district — a Tigrayan tribal stronghold; 17 members of the Ethiophan Evangelical Church; 100 members of the Oromo Libĕration Front; and many, many more. Well over 1,500 people are known to be held in detention without any recourse to normal legal procedures, either at the 'third police' station in Addis Ababa, in Sembel prison, in the Haz-Haz women's prison in Asmara, or in the Mariam Gimbi security prison in the same city. Allegations of torture are widespread but, even without this, prison conditions are not the most pleasant — overcrowding, lack of hygienic or medical facilities, and practical starvation unless relatives bring in food parcels being the norm rather than the exception.

Perhaps Bob Geldof's slogan should have been '*free*' rather than '*feed the world*'?

Ghana
Military Intelligence handles all the functions of a secret police service in Flight Lieutenant Jerry Rawlings' Ghana, and has done ever since his Provisional National Defence Council overthrew the civilian regime of Dr Hilla Limann in December 1981.

Detainees today are principally members of the previous government, or journalists and newspaper editors who have expressed opposition in print to the present government. Instances of brutality are rare, however, and do not appear to be part of state policy. One man, Victor Agbewali, did suffer severe damage to his eyesight after having been beaten in an army barracks following his arrrest on suspicion of possessing a firearm. By contrast, at least three members of the security forces are known to have been executed by firing squad for the murder of prisoners, and today Ghana is a safe country for most of its inhabitants.

Mozambique

Some 5,000 people are known to have been detained in Mozambique following a series of waves of arrests over the last couple of years by the National Security Service. Those arrested are all accused of being active or passive members or supporters of the principal opposition movement which aims to overthrow by force the government of President Samora Machel, the *Resistência Nacional Moçambicana* (RNM). The arrests followed an agreement drawn up in March 1984 with the South African government, known as the 'Nkomati Accord', under which each country agreed that it would no longer harbour resistance fighters aimed against the other. RNM bases in South Africa were closed and the Mozambique government reciprocated by exiling members of the African National Congress from Maputo, the capital.

The National Security Service, whose principal function is the prevention of terrorism, was formed in October 1975 immediately following Mozambique's independence from Portugal. Since then, prior to the most recent clamp-down, the organization has been responsible for many hundreds of arrests, and large numbers of prisoners have been held in detention, often under appalling conditions, for ten years or more. Most political detainees are taken for primary interrogation to the main detention centre at Machava and are later distributed to 're-education' camps in the country.

Among those known to be detained without trial — the Portuguese government abolished *habeas corpus* for political offenders in 1974 and President Machel has maintained the *status quo* — are Victor Naitang, an air force pilot who was arrested in 1981 after a colleague defected to South Africa; and Bidimingo Luis Matchabe, a railway worker who dared to write to the government complaining about arbitrary arrests. Neither is known to have any affiliation with the RNM, and they have simply disappeared alongside thousands of others whose whereabouts and state of health have not been released even to the International Committee of the Red Cross.

Some prisoners, mostly foreign nationals, have been freed in the last couple of years, including 11 Portuguese and a Sri Lankan. Many of those released have subsequently claimed to have been tortured, or to have witnessed other prisoners being tortured by the National Security Service, although such allegations have declined since about 1980. Methods used by the secret police include tying the arms tightly behind the back with wet ropes which contract as they dry, cutting off the circulation and causing unconsciousness followed by agonizing pain as the circulation is restored.

Whipping — public flogging is a legal punishment for many crimes in Mozambique — is also employed. The offences can be as trivial as distributing anti-government leaflets or insulting public officials.

Namibia

Namibia, which includes the notorious Skeleton Coast as well as the Namid and Kalahari Deserts, is still administered by South Africa whose Bureau of State Security (BOSS) is active in attempting to suppress the independence movement, the South-West Africa People's Organization (SWAPO). BOSS is helped in this by a special police counter-insurgency unit known as *Koevoet* (Crowbar) whose methods of interrogation and use of murder are well known. *Koevoet* is principally an Afrikaans organization, as its name suggests, but pro-government blacks are also employed in the covert role to infiltrate SWAPO and lead the armed police to the houses of known members or to secret meetings of dissidents. Retribution on such informers is sharp, swift and brutal when they are discovered, the most primitive forms of torture, including disembowelment, cutting off fingers, toes, ears and genitals, ripping out eyes and tongue and impalement, all being practised. The continuing war in Namibia is fought without quarter being given or expected, and the security forces are ruthless in the application of torture in order to extract information.

Most of the activity takes place in the northern and most densely populated region of the country, particularly in Ovamboland and Kavango provinces which have been under a declared state of emergency since 1979, and where the security police have unlimited powers of arbitrary arrest and detention. Prisoners may be held for indefinite periods of time without being allowed to see a lawyer or even notify their relatives of their plight, and the security forces enjoy legal immunity for any offences they may commit during their investigations, up to and including summary execution.

In an attempt to 'disprove' allegations of torture and murder, the South African government set up a 'model' camp near Mariental to house over 100 men kidnapped during a foray into neighbouring Angola, and invited the International Committee of the Red Cross to send in an inspection team. No such delegations have ever been allowed near any of the other detention centres in the country. . .

In 1982 a report published by the Southern African Catholic Bishops' Conference following visits by two clerical delegations the previous year referred to allegations of torture by means of electric shock devices, beatings, blindfolding and partial suffocation, and commented that it was 'common knowledge' that 'detention and interrogation in any part of the country are accompanied by beating, torture, sparse diet and solitary confinement'. The South African government simultaneously denied the torture charge and banned publication of the report in South Africa or

Namibia! Later the same year two men, Jona Hamukwaya and Kadumu Katanga, are known to have died within hours of having been seized by *Koevoet* and, although an enquiry was held, the only result at the time of writing has been the arrest of Roman Catholic Archbishop Denis Hurley for his public criticism of *Koevoet* and their complicity in Hamukwaya's murder.

Koevoet has been accused by many more people, not least among them being Hans Röhr, leader of the Namibian Christian Democrat Party, who in February 1984 widely publicized the case of a prisoner, Ndara Kapitango, whose arm had to be amputated after he had been badly and deliberately burned by security forces. Röhr has also complained about the executions of a child and five adults during a raid on a village near Nepara, in Kavango province, in August 1984. Once again, an enquiry was promised but no results have ever emerged.

In essence, it is clear that Namibia, in theory at least a semi-independent state, is being used by the South African forces as a 'buffer zone' against aggression through or from Angola and it is improbable that the security forces' stranglehold on the country will be relaxed until the South African regime gives up its rigid and increasingly absurd racial laws in favour of some form of properly administered proportional representation and equal civil liberties for all — or is overthrown in the increasingly likely bloodbath which has been building up for so many years.

Rwanda

All that most people know about Rwanda is that it produces some of the most visually attractive postage stamps in the world — stamps of no value to serious collectors but, like those from several other tiny states, a significant revenue-earner for the government in the form of those 'philatelist starter packs' often advertised wherein you get 500 stamps for £1 or $1. What is not known by the majority of people — principally youngsters — who paste these garish offerings into their albums is that this small African state west of Lake Victoria 'boasts' one of the most repressive regimes in a repressive continent, and that its secret police, the *Service Central de Renseignements* (SCR), which is solely responsible to President Juvénal Habyarimana, is more barbaric and less inhibited in its treatment of suspected political offenders than even those of some of the other countries already discussed.

The SCR's main headquarters are in Kigali, the capital, but the secret police also administer Ruhengeri prison in the north, where many supposed opponents of Habyarimana's regime are detained under conditions of total darkness in tiny cells with neither windows nor artificial lighting. Living under such circumstances for prolonged periods can cause severe deterioration in eyesight as well as other physical and psychological complaints.

Prior to 1980 the man in charge of the SCR was Théoneste Lizinde, and conditions were, if possible, even worse than today. In April of that year, however, Lizinde and some 50 other people were arrested for plotting to overthrow the government, and presumably subjected to the same sort of treatment they were more used to meting out. One man, Stanilslas Biseruka, managed to get away, even though suffering from partial paralysis and a dislocated hip as a result of torture, and sought asylum in Uganda in 1980 (after Idi Amin had been deposed). However, the SCR 'snatched' him in Kampala a year later and returned him to prison. When he appeared in court, accused of conspiring to help overthrow the government, he was able to walk only with the aid of crutches. However, the same court threw out his allegations of torture.

Many other prisoners accused of conspiracy, often on fabricated evidence, have given testimony of severe beatings by the SCR, of electric shock treatment and of having needles inserted under finger- and toenails, as well as of having been forced to endure the psychological nightmare of a mock execution.

South Africa
One word summarizes the reasons for the existence of one of the most skilled and ruthless secret police forces in the world, of the largest and best-equipped army and air force in Africa, and of one of the most effective counter-insurgency units anywhere: that word is, of course, apartheid.

The population of South Africa is composed of some twenty million blacks, three million Asians and 'coloureds' – and five million whites of predominantly Boer or British descent. The country's original inhabitants were the small, yellow-skinned Hottentots and Bushmen. Although the Cape of Good Hope was first sighted by Bartholomew Diaz in 1488, and rounded nine years later by Vasco da Gama, it was not until nearly 200 years later still that Europeans began settling in this land, agriculturally and minerally the richest in all Africa.

The first permanent settlement was established at the Cape by Jan van Riebuck, a ship's surgeon with the Dutch East India Company, in 1652. Within a couple of decades a small but rapidly flourishing community of farmers – burghers — had been established. Already, however, the beginnings of what was to become South Africa's single biggest problem could be seen. Hottentots were captured and kept as slaves and, inevitably, there were sexual liaisons resulting in the first half-caste children, or what are today called 'coloureds'.

Until the Suez Canal was built 200 years later, the Cape was a vital stopping-off place on the route to India and the Far East, so the little Dutch community began to prosper and by the end of the 17th century its population numbered some 2,000 whites and 1,000 slaves. Its numbers had been swelled by Huguenot exiles from France, whose strong Calvinism was to exert a significant effect on the community's religious beliefs and observances. During the 18th century the population gradually split into two groups, those who lived in Cape Town and the *veeboeren*, the Dutch farmers and their families who, in ox-drawn wagons, trekked progressively further into the country's interior in their search for land. Eventually this brought them for the first time into contact with the Bantu tribes who were similarly moving south in their own search for land, and out of the rivalry between them emerged the succession of 'Kaffir wars' which were to continue until the end of the 19th century, when rivalry of a different sort would explode into warfare.

As the 18th century drew to a close, there was increasing resentment among the Afrikaaners, as the Dutch settlers now called themselves, at the restrictive laws imposed upon them by the now-ailing Dutch East India Company, and a growing desire for legal, social and economic independence. What happened, though, was that the Afrikaaners exchanged one set of masters for another.

In 1795 Holland was allied with the Revolutionary government in France which had deposed the Bourbon monarchy, and was therefore at war with England. The community at the Cape had no organized military force and was consequently unable to resist when nine English men-of-war sailed into Table Bay and established a British military government. For a brief period this seemed no bad thing, for the English presence opened up new trade markets for Afrikaaner produce — particularly the famous Cape wines which found a welcome reception in London. The British forces also penetrated into the interior and established for the first time a supposedly neutral zone between the lands held by the Boer farmers and those held by the Bantu tribes. Population pressure — since British settlers soon began to establish themselves in South Africa — and greed would quickly destroy this arrangement.

The trade benefits of British rule were rapidly seen by the Afrikaaners as the proverbial thin end of the wedge during the first decades of the 19th century, as English became the official language of the country and — alongside Latin! — was the only one permitted in schools. Even worse, as far as the Boers were concerned, Britain abolished the slave trade and forced the Afrikaaners to free their Hottentot servants, with little or no compensation. In 1835, therefore, increasing numbers of farmers, particularly from the eastern provinces, began what has entered history as the Great Trek. Pushing ever northwards and further into the interior, the farmers carved out even greater tracts of land for themselves and, inevitably, ran headlong into conflict with the warlike Bantu tribes who naturally resented this incursion into their territory. Mzilikazi and his *impis* of Matabele fought fiercely against this encroachment, but were forced back behind the River Limpopo. However, Dingaan, king of the mighty Zulu empire, having first signed a treaty allowing the settlers land across the Tugela, fell upon them and slaughtered an estimated 300 people. The Boers, under the inspired leadership of Andries Pretorious, rallied and fought back and, at what became known as the battle of Blood River in 1838, killed 3,000 Zulu warriors.

The British government, concerned at these developments, sent troops to annex the new territories which the Boers had settled and christened Natal, Transvaal and the Orange Free State. However, their administration and control proved impossible, and in the mid-1850s they were granted independence. The seeds of conflict between Briton and Boer had been sown, though. Moreover, there were differences in government between the three states which would eventually lead to the schizoid situation of today. Whereas Cape Province and Natal developed democratic parliaments which took no notice of the colour of a man's skin, in the Orange Free State and the Transvaal prejudice was deeply rooted and took the form of the wording in their constitutions that it was the desire of the people 'to permit no equality between the coloured peoples and the white inhabitants, either in church or state'.

In 1867 diamonds were discovered in the Orange Free State, producing a huge influx of a new type of settler, interested not in land but in getting rich. The British government revoked its earlier agreement and reclaimed the diamond-rich territory — the Kimberley fields — for the Crown, provoking further resentment amongst the Afrikaaners. The diamond discovery also produced a new problem, for there was work in the new fields for thousands of black labourers, and this resulted in a new class of 'industrial' blacks, concentrated together in greater density than anywhere else in white-administered southern Africa.

In the second half of the 19th century the British government went even further. Seeing that no real progress towards modernization would ever be made by the group of self-governing and politically different states in southern Africa, the Colonial Secretary, Lord Carnarvon, proposed federation. Since it was precisely rule from Westminster which the Boers had joined in the Great Trek to escape, this plan was met with intense hostility and in 1880 the leaders of the free states, Kruger, Joubert and Pretorious, met to form an executive government and raised the republican flag in defiance of the British. The first Boer War had begun.

In a short campaign the Boers won three engagements against British troops and Prime Minister Gladstone relented and returned internal independence to the Transvaal, although foreign affairs were still to be administered from Whitehall. This concession came too late. Rivalry between Briton and Boer was now firmly established, the Cape Boers who had previously thought little of the political concerns of their neighbours in the free states began to realize that they had more in common with them than with the British, and the cry 'Africa for the Afrikaaners' began to be heard.

Now a new element in the troubled politics of South Africa was introduced. Bismarck, Chancellor of the newly united Germany, proclaimed a German protectorate over most of what is now Namibia, and the British government was naturally concerned about a possible coalition between German and Boer. Anxious to seize as much land as possible before any other European powers also got 'into the act', Britain annexed first Bechuanaland and then Zululand. Meanwhile, gold had been discovered in the Transvaal, on the Witwatersrand, and an influx of settlers anxious for quick wealth took place, just as it had earlier at Kimberley. Almost overnight, from being a relatively poor, agricultural country, the Transvaal became one of the richest in Africa. Although it was not immediately apparent, the inevitable result would be war again.

Cecil John Rhodes, the enigmatic Englishman who had made a huge fortune out of the Kimberley diamond fields, had the dream of an English empire in Africa from the mouth of the Nile to the Cape; as Prime Minister of the Cape, he set about energetically trying to isolate the Transvaal in a sea of English colonies. He also implemented measures to try to integrate the black population more democratically — earlier, many blacks had become disenfranchised due to an inability to read or write. This plan was diametrically opposed to that of the free states — particularly Natal — which sought to keep black and white apart, preserving the tribalism which Rhodes was trying to destroy. Attempting to bring the other South African states into line, Rhodes conceived the plan of using the *uitlanders* — settlers of nationality other than Dutch or British — to foment a revolt. This scheme came to naught in the fiasco known afterwards as the Jameson Raid, and Rhodes himself, his health failing, was discredited. His successor, Sir Alfred Milner, continued to press the idea of the franchise for other nationalities, but ran head on into equal stubbornness from Kruger.

The second Boer War was significant in many ways other than in who won. The Boers used fast-moving commandos in hit-and-run raids, avoiding pitched battle wherever possible. The British troops were forced to abandon their red coats and don khaki. The Boers lived off the land, supported by the farms. The British therefore introduced concentration camps, into which the farming families were herded while their crops were burnt and their cattle seized. It was a costly war for both sides, and the remnants of the bitterness it caused still exist, but after two and a half years the Boers were forced to concede.

It cost Britain £30 million — a huge amount in those days — to rebuild the economy afterwards, but the price was a small one to pay for a united South Africa which was at last a full member of the British Empire. South African troops subsequently fought with zeal and determination on the Allied side in both World Wars. In the inter-war period, however, two events took place of great relevance to the situation in South Africa today. In 1926 the Balfour Declaration made all member countries of the Empire equal in status under the Crown, so there was no longer any question of internal South African politics being dictated by Westminster or Whitehall. The Status of the Union Act of 1934 ratified this. The South African Prime Minister, Hertzog, then introduced the racial legislation which is still so controversial. Cape Africans lost their franchise and were put on a separate electoral register, with powers only to elect three white politicians to parliament to represent them; and a Native Land Trust was established to purchase land for black reservations.

On the outbreak of the Second World War Hertzog supported South African neutrality but was defeated and forced to resign by those, led by Smuts, who wished to side with England. After the war Smuts' coalition government was itself defeated by the Nationalist Party under Dr F. D. Malan, whose platform was apartheid — a policy aimed at much more than just the segregation of races. Coloureds as well as blacks were placed on a separate electoral roll, the country began being split into separate racial zones, mixed marriages and sexual intercourse between people of different races were forbidden, separate buses, waiting rooms, restaurants and other facilities were established for blacks and coloureds, and a separate educational system was inaugurated. These policies have been maintained by Malan's successors to this day, despite growing internal unrest since the 1960s — when South Africa left the Commonwealth — and international concern about the plight of the non-white population which has led to sanctions and boycotts.

Many people, beginning with the British Prime Minister Harold Macmillan, have predicted the downfall of apartheid, especially since the Sharpeville shooting on 3 February 1960 when 69 Africans were killed by government forces, and even more so since the collapse of white rule in Rhodesia, now renamed Zimbabwe. So far, however, the security forces seem to have managed to keep the situation under control, although their methods are far from laudable.

The principal security agency is BOSS, the Bureau of State Security, with headquarters in Pretoria. Its membership is believed to comprise some 18,000 men, and their methods include holding detainees incommunicado, physical assault and torture. In 1982 a new Internal Security Act was passed which gives BOSS almost unlimited powers in controlling terrorism. Prisoners may be held, often in solitary confinement, for an unlimited length of time with no recourse to legal counsel, and are usually denied access to friends or relatives. Many prisoners are subjected to prolonged interrogation, accompanied by beatings and worse forms of torture, in some cases leading to their deaths. Members of BOSS enjoy virtual legal immunity for such crimes. Two security officers brought to trial for the murder of

Riot police in action, South Africa

Tshifhiwa Muofhe in the Venda tribal 'homeland' — actually a native reservation with no status in international law — in 1981 were acquitted by the Supreme Court: an obviously rigged verdict.

Occasionally, however, the judiciary is forced to take note of police offences. In 1979, for example, a Soweto student leader, Linda Mario Mogale, was sentenced to seven years' imprisonment. At an Appeal Court in 1981 he had his sentence revoked when he was able to convince the court that his conviction was based upon a false confession obtained under torture, which included electric shocks and having some of his teeth pulled out with a pair of pliers. Under South African law, however, complaints of brutality or torture against police or security officers must take place within six months of the offence, and since Mogale's appeal came after this period his torturer escaped scot-free.

Similar accusations of torture by BOSS personnel were brought in 1982 during the inquest into the death of a white official of a black trades union. Neil Aggett had been arrested in November 1981 and was found hanged in his cell in Johannesburg security police prison in February 1982. At the inquest, several other detainees called as witnesses said that Aggett had twice complained of having been tortured by electric shock treatment and

Armed with teargas and rubber bullet gun in South Africa.

sleep deprivation, and some said that they themselves had also been similarly treated. It was also revealed at the inquest that Aggett had been continously interrogated for over 60 hours just prior to his death. Despite these allegations the coroner ruled that Aggett's death had not been induced by ill-treatment by BOSS, and accepted police denials that torture had taken place!

Later in 1982 the Detainees' Parents Support Committee, which works to protect the interests and physical safety of those held by the security forces, published a report based upon 70 sworn affidavits from released prisoners which stated that 'systematic and widespread torture is an integral feature of the detention system'. It stated that common methods of torture included electric shock treatment, hooding prisoners so that they almost suffocated, beatings with truncheons, and suspending victims from poles, their wrists handcuffed to their ankles. Many other prisoners were forced to stand for prolonged periods, sometimes holding a heavy weight above their heads. Humiliating methods of interrogation, such as forcing a prisoner to stand naked and denying him use of toilet facilities, are also employed, the report stated.

Deaths in detention are commonplace, some 300 between 1980 and 1982 being reported by Amnesty International, whose latest annual report refers to 'further deaths in detention under suspicious circumstances', but does not give numbers.

In 1984 the government of Prime Minister — now President — P.W. Botha introduced constitutional changes giving coloureds and Asians direct representation in parliamentary assemblies. This produced a continuing outbreak of civil unrest among the blacks, confined to their townships and 'homelands' and having no say in the running of the government. There were, and continue to be, widespread riots and protest rallies which are dispersed by riot police and the paramilitary *Koevoets* (see the section on Namibia) using firearms as well as truncheons. Hundreds of people have been killed or injured in such confrontations.

Hundreds of blacks are imprisoned by the security forces under the 'pass laws' which deny blacks free movement within the country without an official pass. This legislation was introduced to help control terrorist infiltration but has, needless to say, resulted in the arrests of many, many, innocent people.

The sad story could go on indefinitely. Arrests of trades union and church leaders, members of opposition political groups, of journalists and others, continue to be reported on an almost daily basis. Armed police patrol the streets and the army is constantly on the alert. Yet, strangely, the average South African white — especially the Afrikaaner — will deny being a racialist. The Bantu, he will say, is not an inferior being, he is the equal of the white man but at a lower stage of evolution.

Patrolling the streets of Soweto with armoured personnel carrier.

Uganda

When self-styled 'General' Idi Amin was deposed in 1979, many people thought that an end would come to the reign of terror which had lasted for the previous eight years, but this has not proved to be the case and the security forces established by the paranoid and schizophrenic dictator still retain all their old powers.

'I was held down with two soldiers treading on my wrists and legs, and pins were stuck under my toenails . . . The next day we were ordered to crawl over some very sharp stones which cut our hands and knees until they bled. The two in front were ordered to go outside. I heard two shots and then four of us were ordered to go outside too. I thought this was the end but we were just told to load the dead bodies on to a Land Rover.' Thus reads part of the testimony of one prisoner held by the security forces under Amin's rule.

Tens of thousands of people — the lowest estimate is 100,000 and the actual figure may be as high as a quarter of a million — perished at the hands of the security forces during 1971–79. One of the first things Amin did after seizing power from Milton Obote was to create two new secret police agencies, the Public Safety Unit, the executive organization with power to shoot to kill on suspicion; and the innocuous-sounding Bureau of State Research which was the interrogation arm. Both were based at Kampala, in Naguru and Nakasero respectively.

Amin himself was a ruthless, brutal and ignorant man, the son of a witch-doctor. He became a Moslem at the age of 16 and his period in power was characterized by his racialist, pro-Arab attitudes. He had served in the King's Africa Rifles prior to Ugandan independence and was promoted to Colonel by Obote. Appointed in military charge of the north of the country, supported by the Kakwa and Nubi tribespeople who provided his power base, he rapidly built up a vast personal fortune through smuggling and murder. However, when Obote traced £2.5 million of missing government funds to Amin, it was the signal for the coup Amin had already been planning with help from Libya's President Gaddafi and the Palestinian leader Yasser Arafat. Once in power, Amin drew on their further support, and Palestinian terrorists provided his personal bodyguard and also proved most adept at the interrogation of prisoners under torture.

Amin's reign of terror really started in August 1972 when he expelled Uganda's Asian population and seized their property. Under Palestinian and Libyan guidance, the Public Safety Unit arrested and the Bureau of State Research interrogated all known or suspected opponents of the regime, particularly guerrillas acting on behalf of Obote, who was then in exile. The Bureau's headquarters was linked to the presidential palace by a secret underground tunnel along which Amin frequently liked to have prisoners brought to share cocktails with him — a sadistic refinement of

Idi Amin's seventh anniversary address while still in power.

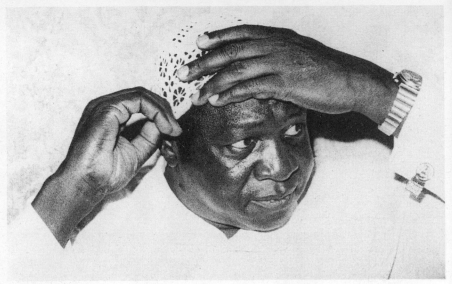

Amin in exile.

torture. Black officials of the secret police were less subtle —
sledge–hammers were their favourite instrument of execution. In some
cases, prisoners had to kill each other. They would be lined up, and one
would be given a sledge–hammer and told to beat a second prisoner to
death. This continued down the line until there was only one victim left,
who would be shot by a guard. Bodies were either dumped in the forests
and rivers or sometimes returned, usually mutilated, to relatives. Other
people, particularly those in prominent positions such as Archbishop
Luwum and cabinet ministers Charles Oboth-Ofumbi and Lieutenant-
Colonel Wilson Oryema, were murdered in faked car accidents.

Amin literally planned genocide, and his security forces eagerly partici-
pated in his plans, arresting, torturing and killing members of the Langi
and Acholi tribes, traditional enemies of Amin's own Lugbara tribe. The
populations of whole villages were slaughtered and their houses looted,
then burned to the ground. Finance for the security forces came from a
variety of sources, including drug smuggling which had covert government
approval.

Most of these facts emerged after Milton Obote, backed by the Tanzanian
army, invaded Uganda in April 1979 and deposed Amin, who fled into
exile, first to Libya, then to Saudi Arabia. Although the mass killings
temporarily stopped, President Obote's National Security Agency, which
took over the functions of the Public Safety Unit and Bureau of State

Research, continued to arrest political opponents and to use torture, including electric shock treatment and beatings with electric cables, in order to extract information or 'confessions'. One of the most shocking of recent cases was that of 18-year-old Annette Nnakandi, who was arrested and tortured before being released, uncharged, two months later. Her eight-month-old daughter was with her throughout the ordeal. Many other innocent people have undergone similar experiences, and in 1984 the American Assistant Secretary of State for Human Rights and Humanitarian Affairs reported that between 100,000 and 200,000 people had been systematically killed by the Ugandan army or allowed to starve to death since 1981. The Ugandan government denied this but admitted to 15,000 — still a shocking indictment.

Zimbabwe

The idyllic state dreamed of by black nationalists when Ian Smith was deposed in 1980 and white rule ceased in Rhodesia has not come to pass. There is fierce political rivalry between Prime Minister Robert Mugabe's ruling ZANU party (Zimbabwe African National Union), former members of the Zimbabwe People's Revolutionary Army (ZIPRA) and the opposition Zimbabwe African People's Union (ZAPU). Most of the armed opposition to Mugabe's government comes from Matabeleland, which has been placed under curfew and its inhabitants prohibited from moving away. The government's principal security agency, the Central Intelligence Organization (CIO), backed by the army's Fifth Brigade, was sent into the area during 1983 and there was a wave of brutal killings. Journalists who managed to get into the area after restrictions were eased in 1984 reported widespread evidence of starvation, for the government had not been allowing food supplies in, as well as the presence of several detention centres and mass graves for prisoners who had died or deliberately been killed during interrogation.

Many long-term prisoners, some of them arrested under the Smith regime, are still in CIO hands, and Bishop Abel Muzorewa was finally released only in September 1984. Others, especially members of ZAPU who have tried to investigate the situation in Matabeleland, such as George Marange and the Reverend Masiyane, have 'disappeared', probably into the main CIO interrogation centre, Stops Camp, inside Mzilikazi Police Station in Bulawayo. At least 12 other people are known to have been condemned to death for armed offences, although only two executions are believed to have been carried out since 1984. It is understood that both President Mugabe and his Minister of Justice are in favour of abolishing the death penalty for criminal offences, but there is widespread opposition, particularly from the military, who favour public execution of guerrillas by firing squad.

CHAPTER SEVEN

NORTH AFRICA AND THE MIDDLE EAST

IRAN · IRAQ · ISRAEL · LIBYA · SYRIA · TURKEY

The Middle East, which for political and ethnic reasons must today be taken to include north African countries such as Libya, has been the centre of modern terrorist activity since the late 1940s. The sheer power held by the few countries in this relatively barren part of the globe due to the huge oil resources without which Western civilization would founder, coupled with religious and racial fanaticism, has produced a revolution in more respects than one. Tighter security controls for international travellers at airports and docks are just the tip of the iceberg. Internal security, and the arrest of anyone remotely suspected of belonging to a terrorist organization — except in those countries such as Libya which openly support such activities — has also been greatly increased. With the exception of Israel, whose security needs are both different and greater, this has led to excesses in which thousands of people have been, and continue to be, arrested, questioned, tortured, incarcerated and executed without trial or any real evidence being presented against them.

What takes place in Iran and Iraq is not restricted to those countries alone — Algeria, Kuwait, Morocco, Tunisia and other states utilize the same methods and for the same reasons, although generally on a smaller scale. To detail the activities of all their secret and military police forces would, however, be to heap unnecessary straws upon the camel's back, so I have restricted this survey to those countries listed above.

Iran

One of the outstanding phenomena of the 1960s and '70s was the sweeping success of Muslim fanatics in Africa and the Middle East, buoyed up by the confidence inspired by deep oil reserves. However, those most inspired were not the orthodox Sunni Moslems as represented by the ruling houses of Jordan and Saudi Arabia, but the extremist groups such as the Shi'ites, Druzes, Ismailis and Alawites, whose cults embrace the twin tenets of puritanism and violence. It was this movement which not only led to the crisis in the Lebanon, the assassination of President Anwar Sadat of Egypt and the destruction of the shrine of Mecca, but also to the overthrow of the Peacock Throne in Iran and the exile of the Shah.

However, it would be wrong to attribute the Shah's fall solely to the fanaticism of the Ayatollah Khomeini and his followers. The Shah's rule had, by Middle Eastern standards, been benevolent, and his policies embraced elements from both communism and capitalism, but the seeds of his 'collective' programme, which aimed to improve levels of agricultural production and share the proceeds among the population fell on the stony ground of peasant farmers. Using his oil revenues, his personal relationships with many of the heads of government around the world, his western education and his increasingly sophisticated middle class population, the Shah tried — and for a time appeared to be succeeding — to drag Iran into the 20th century. However, the Muslim fundamentalists found ready support among the largely uneducated peasants who did not understand, or really want, the changes their ruler planned. As a result, the Ayatollah's campaign succeeded, the Peacock Throne was overturned, and Iran has reverted to medieval barbarism.

One of Khomeini's first moves was to terrorize and destroy anyone sympathetic to the Shah's regime, but he did not stop there. Rival ayatollahs who might, together, have formed an opposition party were ruthlessly hunted down and killed. So were the leaders of ethnic and religious minorities, including Kurds, Turkomans, Jews, Christians, Sunni Moslems and others. Iraq is a Sunni state, and the Ayatollah's persecution, which was followed by corresponding arrests and killings of Shi'ites in Iraq in reprisal, led to the continuing war between the two countries. All this has happened in the last seven years.

In Iran today, the *Pasadaran*, or Revolutionary Guards, fulfil all the functions of a secret police organization, although there is little secret about their aims or methods. No one who does not fully support the Ayatollah Khomeini is free from their suspicion, and their arrests are as frequently to coerce religious 'conversions' out of people as to produce 'confessions' of anti-government activity. In this sense the *Pasadaran* are probably closer to the historical Inquisition than any other secret police force in the world today; certainly their motivation is primarily religious and less concerned

Iraqi prisoners of war — casualties of the conflict with Iran.

with secular opposition than in the vast majority of other countries.

One man who eventually succeeded in escaping from *Pasadaran* custody, but who now lives in hiding, has given the following account of his arrest and subsequent treatment. He was, and is, a member of the People's *Mujahedin* Organization which seeks the overthrow of the present regime.

'I was searched and blindfolded and put in a cell with my hands tied behind me. I was beaten with cables from midday to the evening while they interrogated me. One of the first things they did was to play football with me. Still blindfolded, with my hands bound, I was pushed and beaten, punched and kicked from one guard to the next. This football game is often used on people who have just been arrested. It breaks down the resistance, and can make one feel lonely and unstable. I received the same treatment, and the interrogation continued, for four days, and the next morning I was taken from my cell, blindfolded and with my hands still tied. They wrapped a blanket round me and tied it in place with ropes and covered me with a sack. I was put in the back of a van to be transferred to my home town. During the journey two guards beat me, and taunted me by asking why I didn't try to escape, and threatened me with execution. We arrived at midday and they left me in the courtyard in the hot sun. Later they fetched me and removed the blanket, and the beatings began again.

'After I had gone to the Prosecutor's office, they put metal handcuffs on my hands: the kind which have serrated edges and which tighten their grip if you move. I remained handcuffed for more than a month — the only time they were removed was after ten days, when my hands were bound in front instead of behind my back. I had to eat my food while wearing them, which was very demoralizing, and also while going to the toilet.

'During torture sessions the handcuffs would tighten, and the wounds on my wrists became infected.'

The prisoner was transferred to a new cell 'which was completely water-logged as rain drained from the roof of the building into the cell. There was only one chair and I spent all my time sitting on that chair. I couldn't lie down to sleep on the floor because of the water, and my movements were very restricted because of the handcuffs. The interrogations continued, and they told me to repent and confess on television. The beating was different this time. Before, it had been fairly haphazard, intended to frighten or disorientate, and was applied to all parts of my body, but now it was much more systematic. They find out your weak spot and then concentrate on that. For example, they stripped me and laughed to see how I reacted to that kind of humiliating treatment. They beat me repeatedly on the feet with a thick electric cable, and from time to time would pour cold water on my feet and then start again. They continued for hours. The beating was the most painful thing, the hardest to bear, and I often lost consciousness.

'The next day two guards held my hands and two others my feet. They raised me up and then dropped me on the floor. One of them jumped on to my stomach, and I felt something snap in my back. Then I fainted. During that month, apart from the beating, I was burned with lighted cigarettes and my fingers were crushed together after a pencil was inserted between them. I was also suspended by my wrists from the ceiling for ten hours, and subjected to a mock execution.'

After a month of such treatment the prisoner had lost a great deal of weight, was extremely weak and in a great deal of pain. He was unable to walk, and had to crawl. Eventually he managed to catch the attention of a doctor, who said he should have been in hospital. He was transferred — not to hospital but to the criminal as opposed to the political block of the prison, and his handcuffs were finally removed. After several weeks, and following a sentence of death, he somehow managed to escape — the means cannot be revealed because others may need to use them. Today, five years after his ordeal, the marks of those handcuffs have still not completely faded from his wrists.

Few people arrested in Iran, either by the *Pasadaran* or by the ordinary police, the *komiteh*, are ever sure why they should have been selected. The case above is rare in that the victim was a self-confessed member of a

Hussein Dadhar's feet were crippled by repeated beatings to the soles.

revolutionary group. Most prisoners are never charged, or have any recourse to a 'proper' trial. Such trials as are held in public are normally conducted by a judge whose principal qualifications are religious, in the presence of numerous armed guards, and are over in a matter of a few minutes. A typical example of this form of treatment is shown in the following narrative where, again, the victim has to be anonymous for reasons the reader will respect.

'I was arrested in August 1981, while driving in town. I was blindfolded and taken to the local *komiteh* building and put in a cell with three others. The window was covered up and, when I tried to look outside the door, a guard informed me that if I wished to leave I should name my political contacts. I was treated better than the others initially: I was given a good meal and generally treated well, but the interrogator told me to tell everything I knew.

'When I was on my way to the toilet I saw a man coming towards me with very swollen feet. I was shocked and didn't understand. I asked him what had happened, but a guard interrupted and hit me hard in the face. I was blindfolded and pushed into a room with four or five guards who played football with me for ten to twenty minutes, during which time I was severely beaten.'

The victim, a homosexual, was severely abused both in a 'normal' sexual sense and by being repeatedly kicked in the testicles, so I have deliberately omitted part of the remaining testimony.

'I remained in the same prison for 15 days, during which guards threatened me with execution, and to tell my family that I was in possession of heroin or weapons. I was also subjected to prolonged whippings until I fainted. I was twice subjected to mock execution. One evening, I was taken by car to an unknown place. I was blindfolded and my hands were tied behind my back. I was told that I was to be executed unless I named my friends, in which case I would be released. The guards discussed how to kill me, and asked me if I would prefer to be executed quickly or slowly. I said "quickly", but the guards then disagreed, saying that they preferred to kill me slowly, in stages. Then they discussed whether to kill me there and then or to return me to the prison to be hanged, and whether or not I should remain blindfolded. Finally, they fired shots around me. I was deeply shocked and confused, but then realized that I had not been hit but had been the victim of a mock execution. . . .

' . . . afterwards I was unable to urinate for 24 hours. The next day, still blindfolded, I asked the guard for permission to go to the toilet, and he told me to take three paces forward and one to the right. Following these instructions, I fell from a height of four to five metres [13 to 16 feet] while the guards laughed. I broke two teeth and badly damaged my knee. . .

'I received a visit from relatives only after four months in detention, and was tried (my trial lasted only five minutes) after seven months. I was accused of giving assistance to others who had taken up arms against the Islamic Republic.'

Sentenced to ten years' imprisonment, this man was released after only fifteen months. He was one of the 'lucky' ones in the Ayatollah Khomeini's thoroughly evil regime.

Iraq

One day in September 1982 two security officials called at the home of a woman who must remain nameless to preserve her own life. 'Go to the city mortuary and collect the carcase of your son,' she was told. Ten months earlier her son, a fourth-year medical student from Basra, had been arrested at college along with several other students. Eventually, his mother discovered that he was being held in Abu Ghraib Khassa, the security wing of Baghdad prison. The news of his death was the first she had heard of him for six months.

The following day she went to the mortuary, where about 150 other people were also gathered to claim the bodies of relatives. 'At last I was called in to look for my son and take him away. When I entered and saw what was inside, I could not believe that there are people who could do such things to other human beings.' Her son was lying on the floor in a foetal position alongside nine other corpses. 'He had blood all over him and his body was very eaten away and bleeding. I looked at the others stretched out on the floor alongside him . . . all burnt . . . I don't know what with . . . another's body carried the marks of a hot domestic iron all over from his head to his feet . . . another one was burnt in such a way, even his hair, like someone who has been incinerated . . . and every one was burnt in a different way.

'One of them had his chest cut lengthwise into three sections . . . from the neck to the bottom of the chest was slit with what must have been a knife and the flesh looked white and roasted as if cooked. Another had his legs axed with an axe . . . his arms were also axed. One of them had his eyes gouged out and his nose and ears cut off. One of them looked hanged . . . his neck was long . . . his tongue was hanging out and fresh blood was oozing from his mouth.

'On the same day someone else from our neighbourhood was collecting the body of his nephew, also a fourth-year medical student. He found in the room the bodies of 20 young women, all naked and their breasts cut off. This situation goes on daily at the mortuary. Everyone who goes there mentions that large crowds collect daily and many bodies are taken away.'

Iraq has been at war with Iran for several years and there is considerable opposition to President Saddam Hussain's regime, from members of the Kurdish Democratic Party, from the Patriotic Union of Kurdistan, the Iraqi

Communist Party and the *al-Da'wa al-Islamiyya*, or Islamic Call movement. Nevertheless, the barbarities committed by the Iraqi secret police in their ruthless suppression of political or ethnic dissidents are almost beyond belief.

Two former prisoners, one a Tunisian, the other an American, have not been shy about giving testimony following their release from Abu Ghraib Khassa, and that of Neiji Bennour, the 36-year-old reception manager at the Baghdad Novotel hotel has been widely publicized. Arrested in June 1983, when a colleague lured him out into the hotel's car park where security police were waiting to bundle him into the boot of a car, he was detained under atrocious conditions until April 1984 when urgent appeals by Amnesty International to the Iraqi Ministers of the Interior and Foreign Affairs finally secured his release. For ten months he shared a cell approximately 30 feet wide and 40 feet long with some 200 other prisoners. Lentil soup, beans, rice and bread formed his sole diet throughout his period of detention. He was interrogated under torture at least a hundred times, sometimes two or three times a day, and will carry the physical and mental scars for the rest of his life. Formerly athletic and a keen football player, he now has difficulty in walking because of the repeated blows to the soles and sides of his feet, a form of torture known in the Middle East as *falaqa*; he has a heart condition and cannot bear to sleep alone, frequently screaming from nightmares, according to his wife.

Robert Spurling, a 50-year-old American, was technical director of the same hotel at which Neiji Bennour worked. He was arrested by two security policemen in the departure lounge of Baghdad airport, whence he was intending to fly for a holiday in France, in June 1983 and detained for three and a half months.

He was taken out of the airport to a parked car, blindfolded and driven to what can only have been Abu Ghraib Khassa. After being stripped and issued with a prison uniform, he was put into a comparatively comfortable cell on his own, with two blankets (but no mattress); there was a toilet and shower in the cell, with running hot water.

Mr Spurling was interrogated on 15 occasions, accused of being a spy. 'On 6 July, 23 July and 14 September, I was given 40 blows with a *matraque* [a rubber truncheon] on the soles of my feet, electric shocks were applied to my hands, feet, kidney region, genitals and, above all, to my ears, blows with the forearm to my head, four blows with a rubber truncheon on the upper part of my feet, two blows to my ears with boot heels, blows to the ears with cushions resembling boxing gloves and violent slaps.'

On another occasion he was threatened with mutilation if he did not confess, a scalpel being held against his ear. Examination by a doctor after Mr Spurling returned to America following his release provided evidence of injuries to his feet, hands and to the base of his spine consistent in all ways with his testimony.

Another former prisoner, a 44-year-old Iraqi citizen who wishes for obvious reasons to remain anonymous, described conditions in Abu Ghraib. 'The cells are 2 × 3.5 metres [6.6 × 11.6 feet], very dark and completely covered in red-brown tiles. These cells were really intended for one person and for short periods of interrogation but in fact are used for long periods with up to 18 people at one time. In some of these small cells, people have been detained for several years . . . a shower and open toilet are built into each cell . . . cold water is only turned on once a week for a couple of hours . . . there are no visits from relatives, no correspondence and absolutely no information for the relatives of the whereabouts of the prisoners.

'There are some large cells with an area of approximately 50 square metres [61 square yards]. One of these is specifically for female prisoners. With mass arrests or shortage of space the long corridors on both floors are also used. Steel poles are welded between the cell doors on both sides of the corridor at a height of about 20 cm [eight inches] from the floor and the prisoners are handcuffed by one hand to these poles. In each of these large cells there are 80 to 130 prisoners, sometimes as many as 200. There is only one shower and an open lavatory for all of them. The air is foul and in order to sleep prisoners have to periodically swap places with each other.

'Approximately half of the prisoners were tortured. There are different methods of torture carried out in the torture chambers in the basement. At the entrance to the torture chamber there is a doormat with "Welcome" written on it in English. Torture takes the form of electric shocks; gas and cigarette burns; electric hot plates; hanging from the ceiling — handcuffed; being stretched on a special machine with hands and feet bound; beatings with a heavy cable or high-pressure hose. The tortured prisoners, who are usually unconscious, are then simply carried back to their cells and dumped on the floor in full view of their fellow prisoners.'

Further forms of torture revealed by other released prisoners include an 'electric chair' with five bars which burn the back of the victim; tying prisoners to a spit over an open fire; and sexual abuse of both men and women. Apart from members of the Kurdish nationalist movements and others mentioned earlier, the majority of prisoners today are deserters from the armed forces who oppose the continuing war against Iran.

Israel

As a country which has been under a state of siege since it came into existence in 1947, Israel has been obliged to develop a highly efficient security system, particularly to guard against Palestinian terrorists operating from the Gaza strip, Lebanon and elsewhere. What is little known is that the Jews in the British Protectorate of Palestine had developed a highly

Ethiopian Jews demonstrate in Israel.

effective intelligence service, known as *Shai*, even before that date. *Shai* operated against both the British and the Palestinian Arabs and there was hardly a Jew in what is now Israel who did not cooperate in providing information, surveillance, couriers and armed action squads.

In Israel today there are five principal security agencies: *Aman*, the Bureau of Military Intelligence; the well-known — indeed, one could say infamous — *Mossad*, which is responsible for external security and, for example, for providing armed guards on all *El Al* airliners; *Ran*, the department of counter-espionage; the Research Division of the Foreign Ministry, which analyses information obtained through 'legitimate' sources such as embassy attachés and foreign newspaper reports; and finally the one with which this book must primarily concern itself, *Shin-Beth*, the Department of Internal Security. However, all five departments cooperate at all levels and, due to the nature of the threat facing the very existence of Israel, there are no hard and fast demarcation lines between them. Because of the cosmopolitan nature of the Israeli population, there is no shortage of specialists for particular security assignments either, and a request circulated through the five departments for a left-handed redhead fluent in Swahili who knows the back streets of Cape Town would soon produce a suitable candidate!

The principal purpose of terrorism is to terrorize. This seems so obvious yet is so often forgotten that it needs restating. The reciprocal is that those guilty of terrorism are themselves susceptible to the threat of counter-terrorism. *Shin-Beth* uses counter-terrorism to its limits. The Israeli philosophy is basically one which says 'we are here and we are here to stay. Attack us, bomb us, send infiltrators equipped with bombs to blow up our mothers and our children in our streets, do what you like. We will survive.'

For many Arabs — even those who have adopted Israeli nationality and carry Israeli passports — *Shin-Beth* has a very unsavoury image. The security forces quite legitimately deal forcibly and effectively with Palestinian activists who are caught using violence in furtherance of their aims, but there have been many reported instances — not least from Lebanon — of excessive measures being used against people with no proven connection with terrorists other than that they sympathize with their aims. This, of course, raises the knotty question of whether one can sympathize truly with a cause, and even actively support it through word-of-mouth or written propaganda, without supporting — at least tacitly — its methods. Many civil rights organizations believe that a person can identify with aims and deplore the violence often used in their furtherance: the Israeli Defence Forces do not think this way.

For example, a bookshop proprietor from Gaza was accused and sentenced to a year's imprisonment merely for displaying a poster depicting the Palestinian flag and for stocking 'banned' books by Palestinian authors.

In his defence, Mahmud Muhammad Al Gharbawi said that he had asked the authorities for a list of banned titles but had been told no such document existed. However, he was still sentenced. . .

One cause of concern to many people during the prolonged fighting in Lebanon from which Israel had — at the time of writing — withdrawn, was that people detained in Israeli internment camps had no legal rights. They were not held as prisoners of war, nor were they accused of any crimes in most cases, yet they were denied access to legal advice. However, the International Red Cross were admitted to these camps and no testimony of actual ill-treatment has emerged that I have read.

Within Israel and the so-called 'occupied territories' there exists, it must be said, police power of arbitrary arrest under which suspected terrorists may be held incommunicado for up to 18 days without being charged, and there have been many accounts of prisoners being beaten, deprived of sleep, kept hooded and threatened with physical harm to themselves and their families. However, outwardly at least, the Israeli authorities are concerned about the abuse of such powers and literally dozens of civil and military police officers have been tried and convicted of physically assaulting or otherwise harming or humiliating prisoners over the last couple of years. Most of those convicted, though, receive either suspended sentences or terms of less than six months' imprisonment. . .

Libya

Colonel Mu'ammar Gaddafi (or Gadaffi, Gaddafy or Qaddafi) is yet another of the deranged and fanatical Muslim leaders to have been thrown up in Africa and the Middle East over the last couple of decades in company with Idi Amin and the Ayatollah Khomeini. He came to power in 1969 during a military coup and rapidly replaced President Nasser of Egypt (who died of a heart attack in 1970) as the Pan-Arabic and anti-Israeli, anti-Western leader in north Africa. Using his country's oil reserves — the greatest in the continent west of the Suez Canal — as a weapon against the West, he has made a haven in Libya for terrorist organizations from around the world and, during the 1970s, sought by means of war to convert the whole of Chad to his way of thinking.

Gaddafi's regime is an evil one by any standards and he personally is one of those occasional historical figures, like Hitler, whom many people regret not having had assassinated before he could seize sufficient power to do so much harm. Unfortunately, Gaddafi's own talent for organizing assassinations extends beyond the borders of his own country so that, while internal conditions for his own people are little dissimilar to those already seen in Iran and Iraq, the long arm of the Libyan secret police extends even further abroad.

Fact: Salem Rtemi, a Libyan businessman residing in Italy, disappeared

Libyan leader Colonel Gaddafi

in February 1980 and his bullet-riddled body was found in the boot of his car in Rome a few weeks later.

Fact: Muhammed Mustapha Ramadan, a journalist and open critic of Gaddafi's regime, was shot dead in London's Regent's Park in April 1980. (Two Libyan suspects were later charged with murder and sentenced to life imprisonment.)

Fact: Abduljalil Aref, a Libyan businessman living in Italy, was shot in the head while sitting in a café in the via Veneto, Rome, in April 1980.

Fact: Abdul Rahman Bubaker, a factory worker in his early 20s who had left Libya because of his anti-Gaddafi views after serving a stint in the army, was found with his throat cut in his home in Athens in May 1980. His murderer had inscribed in Arabic on the wall the words 'The revolution will live forever. Death and no mercy to the imperialists.'

Fact: In October 1982 the Libyan government paid an American Marine Corps veteran called Eugene Tafoya £4,210 to assassinate Faisal Zagalli, a 35-year-old Libyan student at Colorado State University. Zagalli was an outspoken critic of the Gaddafi regime and had been living in America for ten years. Earlier he had refused a summons to return to Libya to serve in the army.

Tafoya, who was known to have connections with a former CIA agent called Wilson who is wanted by the American authorities for training terrorists and smuggling arms to Libya, failed in the murder attempt, but Zagalli was wounded and lost an eye. Tafoya was tried and sentenced to two years' imprisonment.

The day after the assassination attempt, the main news station in Tripoli broadcast the following message: 'Confirming that physical liquidation is the final stage in the revolutionary dialectic, called for when economic, political and social weapons fail to put an end to the activities of counter-forces, a member of the international revolutionary committee has tried to liquidate one Faisal Zagalli, who was seriously wounded. Zagalli had studied at the expense of the government for ten years at the American Colorado University to prepare for a master's degree and a doctorate. But instead of returning home to serve his country and people, he became an agent and a spy for American intelligence, supplying it with information about his country.'

In March 1977 Colonel Gaddafi had declared his intention of creating a society in which all conventional forms of authority would be given up and 'people's power' declared. All the traditional institutions were replaced by people's congresses and committees, and even abroad embassies were renamed 'people's bureaux'. These changes, leading to a society comparable to that of China under the Red Guards, were not universally popular, and in 1979 Gaddafi said that the movement was to move from 'the area of motivation to the area of enforcement'. In other words, those who opposed the changes would be forced to comply. Then, in February 1980, the Third Congress of the Libyan Revolutionary Committees called for the physical liquidation of 'enemies of the revolution' living abroad and of any who obstructed 'revolutionary change' within the country.

Prior to this declaration, there had been few reports of torture or 'disappearances' in Libya, but since 1980 these have greatly multiplied. Military Intelligence headquarters in Tripoli is where most prisoners are taken for initial interrogation designed to produce 'confessions' and evidence against other opponents of the People's Congress. Those arrested endure similar conditions to those already described for several other countries. They are held incommunicado, often in solitary confinement, and interrogation is accompanied by beatings, whippings, electric shock treatment, sexual abuse and mock executions.

In July 1982 three students, Saleh Al Kounayti, Ahmed Ismail Maklouf and Naji Bahouia, were executed after having been tortured following a demonstration at Benghazi University, and this was not an isolated example. The long arm of the revolutionary committees even reaches abroad, as we have seen, and in November 1982 two Libyans living in West Germany were abducted off the street and taken to the Libyan People's Bureau in Bonn where they were held for 24 hours and forced to sign 'confessions' after being repeatedly kicked and beaten. Those responsible were arrested by the German police but never sentenced since they were exchanged for eight West Germans detained in Libya.

During 1984 Gaddafi's reign of terror intensified following an attack on his headquarters on 8 May, and hundreds of people were rounded up as suspects. The Libyan authorities make no attempt to hide their activities, and detainees are often paraded on television, their faces cut and bruised from obvious beatings, in order to broadcast their 'confessions'. Nor are visitors to the country immune. On 13 May 1984 a Norwegian sailor, Bjorn Pedersen, was seized and taken to a customs house in Tripoli for interrogation after his cargo ship had been detained by the Libyan authorities, its crew accused of spying and drug smuggling. His shipmates never saw him alive again and the ship was released only after its owners had paid an indemnity of $277,000.

Syria
'I was blindfolded and taken to the interrogator's room and asked about my relationship with X and his connection with the organization of the Muslim Brotherhood. I denied any knowledge of this, whereupon the prison warders were ordered to take me to the torture chamber and beat me.' Thus begins the testimony of a Syrian doctor, a general practitioner, who was arrested with another man, referred to as X, and held in detention by the Syrian secret police for 29 months from 1979 to 1982.

'They dragged me along the ground, stripped and handcuffed me and put me in the *dullab* [a tyre suspended from the ceiling]. Then they beat my feet with electric cables until they became swollen and started bleeding. The interrogator then ordered them to bring me back to his room, so they dragged me along the floor and thrust me in front of him. He repeated the same questions and I gave him back the same answers. I was taken back to the torture chamber and tortured continuously for two hours. The interrogator then ordered that I be taken to the cell.'

Only three hours later the doctor was taken back to the torture chamber. 'There, they removed my handcuffs, stripped me and put me in the *dullab*. They placed electric wires on my hands and feet. They started beating me and turned on the electric current. I screamed. The interrogator came into the room. He repeated his questions and asked me to confess or else I would die under torture. He continued torturing me for several hours and then summoned the doctor who was present at the branch [of the prison]. The doctor examined me and . . . told the interrogator that my condition had deteriorated and that I would not be able to withstand much more. So the interrogator ordered that I be returned to my cell.'

Next morning the interrogation was resumed. 'The torturers beat me all over my body, from head to toe. As a result, my head swelled up, I became blind in one eye and my body was covered with wounds. On this occasion they also turned on the electric current and used an electric iron. Evidence of this torture is still apparent on my body.'

The doctor was taken to al-Mezze military hospital for treatment before being returned to the prison for further interrogation after only two days. This continued for three weeks before he and other prisoners were taken to Tadmur military prison. The doctor was eventually released after he agreed to become a secret police informer, but instead he fled the country and now lives in western Europe. His companion, against whom he was asked to give testimony, was executed.

After his escape, the doctor was given a medical examination which revealed permanent damage to an eye caused by blows from an iron bar, as well as other marks on his feet consistent with his testimony. He also gave evidence about conditions in Tadmur prison, which was infested with flies, lice and rats. The food was frequently rotten and prisoners allowed only two or three baths a year. Scabies and dysentery were commonplace, tuberculosis was widespread and there were outbreaks of cholera and typhoid. Medical care was non-existent and summary executions, for no apparent reasons, took place quite regularly.

The big question is 'why?'. One of the answers is that the Arab world is so divided internally, just like the Christian church was in earlier centuries over religious schisms, that it is difficult to see a solution to their differences in the immediate or even intermediate future. Another is that President

Hafez al-Assad wanted to assume the mantle of Arab leadership after the death of Gamal Nasser of Egypt and the accession of Anwar Sadat, whose appeasement programme in respect of Israel was as little liked in hard-line Arab circles as it was welcomed and applauded in the rest of the world. This, not least because Syria is a predominantly Shi'ite Muslim country, whose messianic belief and addiction to violence (the original 'Assassins' were Shi'ites) are diametrically opposed to the beliefs and traditions of the Sunni Muslims, led to a large part of the tragedy in the Lebanon as well. Syria is a country divided against itself and only the most ruthless methods of repression prevent for the time being the backlash which must, inevitably, come.

The situation can be summarized in a nutshell by the simple observation that, regardless of the external war, Syria has fought against Israel both directly and indirectly (in the Lebanon), the entire country has been under a permanent state of internal emergency for no fewer than 24 years. Under such a climate, any secret police force prospers and its powers become greater — which is exactly what has happened.

As in Iran and Iraq, anyone who opposes the government by word or deed is immediately a suspect traitor and can expect a knock on the door in the middle of the night or a car to pull up alongside them in the street during broad daylight. Again, there is no recourse to legal justice, no access to relatives or friends; detainment is at the discretion of the police or the military and can last from hours to years without trial; torture during interrogation is widespread and, apart from the methods described in the doctor's testimony above, includes use of the *al-'Abd al Aswad* or 'black slave', a horrific device into which the victim is strapped in a sitting position and which then automatically inserts a red-hot skewer up his or her rectum. There is also the *Bisat al-Rih* or 'flying carpet', a wooden silhouette of a human figure to which victims can be strapped, stripped naked with arms and legs extended, so that beatings or electrodes can be applied to any part of the body at the torturer's whim.

Among those known to be held in Syrian security prisons are the First Secretary of the Communist Party, Riad al-Turk; a member of the Party for Communist Action, Fateh Jamus; and the First Secretary of the Syrian League for the Defence of Human Rights, Muwaffaq al-Din al-Kozbari; all of whom have had to spend prolonged periods in hospital following torture sessions. Many hundreds of other people are known to be held in detention in Tadmur prison and elsewhere; dozens of others have simply disappeared, and executions — including public hangings — are almost daily occurrences somewhere in the country. President Assad has a great deal to answer for.

Turkey
It has always seemed to me ironic that Turkey, sharing borders with Iran,

Prisoners being exercised in Mamak Prison, Turkey, 1984.

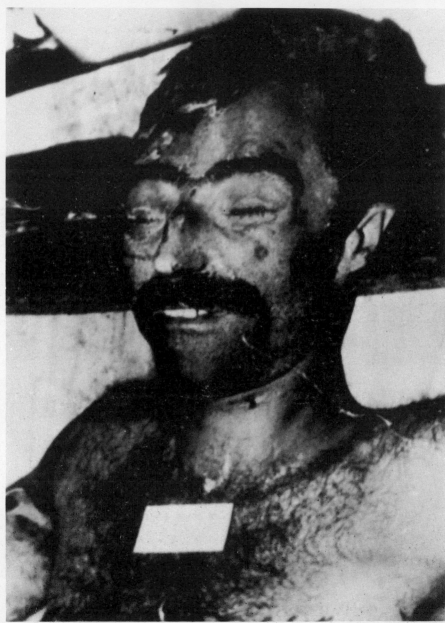

A victim of Turkish torture, Suleyman Cihan.

Iraq and Syria, with many similar ethnic and religious problems, is usually today classified as part of Europe, largely because of its membership of NATO and vital role on the southern flank of the Alliance. For the purposes of this book, and not least because the military police — who perform the work of an internal secret police — utilize much the same methods as those already described for Iran, Iraq and Syria, I have chosen to treat Turkey as part of the Middle East.

Repression, torture, political killings and 'disappearances' were far from unknown even before the military coup of September 1980 which brought Prime Minister Turgut Özal to power. Since then, however, they have multiplied drastically, and at least 20,000 people — probably a conservative estimate — are today known to be held in military or civil prisons for political offences, including membership of Kurdish nationalist groups or the Communist Party.

The reasons, however, are not hard to find. During the five years preceding the coup, at least 5,000 people had been killed in political assassinations by fanatics of both the right and the left, and a state of emergency covered many of Turkey's 67 provinces. Hundreds of those responsible have subsequently been arrested; some have been tried and convicted, many to sentences of execution; more have been questioned and then sent to one of Turkey's several prisons, of which the most notorious are Mamak, Erzurum and Iskenderun; others have been tortured and killed during the course of military police investigations.

Pasa Uzun, now aged 33, was one of some 200 student teachers arrested after the political party to which he belonged was banned by the government *before* the 1980 coup. Following the change in government he was brought to trial, but was barely able to speak due to the ordeal he had been through, which on one occasion included being hung suspended by his ankles for no fewer than 22 days. Pasa Uzun is still a prisoner, in another of Turkey's prisons — Diyarbakir — and has been tortured on several occasions following his conviction. Necmiye Bekel, a Communist, was arrested in July 1981 and had a miscarriage as a result of the beatings administered. She was among another group of some 200 detainees who went on trial in 1982.

Unlike the situation in most other countries, where torture forms part of the interrogation and general 'softening-up' process in the days immediately following arrest, in Turkey torture is a regular part of normal prison life, even following conviction, when 'confessions' are no longer needed. A former prisoner at Mamak said that 'Morning and evening inspections were the scene for daily beatings. They hit you for the slightest infringement of the rules. These beatings took place in the presence of the prison doctor, who was on the inspection team.'

After arrest, most prisoners find themselves in the 'cage' — a literal open cage with iron bars — where they are repeatedly beaten until they can barely move. Once in prison, similar treatment continues, with the added refinement of solitary confinement for a fortnight or more in a tiny cell without a toilet, for those who continue to oppose the regime. Nizamettin Kaya was arrested in 1982 on suspicion of belonging to a Kurdish nationalist group. After his eventual release he testified that he was kicked, beaten with truncheons and canes all over his body, including the soles of his feet, and manacled to hot radiators in corridors where every passing official could throw a blow at him.

'My feet were swollen and even burst and cracked in places. [They] forced my feet into my shoes . . . Afterwards they told me to jump on each foot a hundred times. I could not, so they kept beating me with the truncheon on the head. I was desperate . . . I tried to jump . . . They kicked me on the legs and stepped with their heels on my toes, squashing them.'

Men and women alike suffer under Turkey's barbaric legal and political system. Gulham Tomak was exactly 16 when she was arrested and put into a dormitory with 17 other women, aged from 15 to 50, in Iskenderun Martial Law Compound. 'A 15-year-old girl was paralysed,' Gulhan said afterwards, 'as a result of what she had seen. The others were trying to help her walk. The police were after the sons of a 55-year-old woman. They could not find them so they were holding and torturing the mother instead. Her arm was broken due to these tortures. The wrist of a 19-year-old girl had burst open due to continuous beatings with the truncheons. She was trying to bandage her wrist with the help of some other women.'

Mock crucifixions, in which the victim is tied to a wooden cross while electrodes or hot electric irons are applied to various parts of his or her body, are also common in Turkey's notorious prisons, while in some institutions it is almost considered a luxury to be 'merely' beaten with truncheons instead of pickaxe handles or iron chains.

Kurds, Christians and other members of minority religious or ethnic groups, trades unionists and those belonging to left-wing — especially Communist — organizations are routinely subjected to interrogation under torture in Turkey, and one wonders at the ambivalent attitudes of those politicians and others who will welcome such a country into the North Atlantic Treaty Organization for pragmatic reasons while, for example, simulatenously applying sanctions against South Africa . . .

Pro-government demonstration in Green Square, Tripoli.

CHAPTER EIGHT

ASIA AND AUSTRALASIA
AFGHANISTAN. CHINA. INDIA. INDONESIA. KAMPUCHEA. PHILIPPINES. SRI LANKA

Over such a vast area as this, only a selection of the most culpable secret police forces can be made. China, which today is in a more stable state and administered by a more enlightened government than at any time in its long recorded history, is the 'odd man out' for, although it continues to have a secret service long after the terrors of the 'Cultural Revolution' have ended, it is a country today where most people can get on with their ordinary lives without fear of arbitrary arrest. However, the recent history of China deserves brief examination in a book of this nature and it is included to avoid readers questioning its absence. Other countries which do have secret police forces and which employ repressive methods, such as the use of menaces and torture, include Bangladesh, North and South Korea, Pakistan and Taiwan. The countries covered in this chapter are those where the activities of the secret police are most violent and affect the lives of most people. In some cases hundreds of thousands of people have been killed under the most appalling circumstances in recent years, and the imprisonments, the torture and the executions continue to this day.

Afghanistan
Since 1979 the Soviet-backed puppet government of Afghanistan led by Babrak Karmal has waged a ruthless campaign against the anti-communist guerrillas who continue to control the rugged countryside and make movement outside the major towns perilous — particularly to Russian military

convoys. Apart from the military forces, Karmal has at his disposal the dreaded *Khedemat-e Atla't Dawlati* (*Khad*), or State Information Service, one of the most ruthless of the world's secret police services. The extent of their activities can be appreciated from the fact that there are no fewer than eight secret detention and interrogation centres in Kabul alone where prisoners are routinely tortured by the use of electric shock treatment, by brutal beatings and by sleep deprivation in solitary confinement.

In 1980 several hundred students — including schoolchildren as young as 12 — were arrested following anti-Soviet demonstrations at Kabul University. Many were held for up to four days and subsequently reported that they had been tortured in order to extract information about links with the guerrillas. Some students even had fingernails pulled out with pliers.

Arrests by plain clothes *Khad* squads follow time-honoured practice and usually occur in the dead of night, suspects being hustled from their beds to the secret police headquarters in Sharsh-Darak (a district in Kabul) or to the Central Interrogation Office (*Sedarat*) in the office of the Prime Minister himself. Relatives are forbidden access and prisoners are regularly detained without being charged and without any recourse to legal aid or representation.

A typical case is that of 22–year-old medical student Farida Ahmadi, who was seized in 1981 and incarcerated in a *Khad* detention centre for six months. After her release she escaped from Afghanistan and testified to having been subjected to prolonged interrogation. She was not allowed to sleep for periods of up to a week and was subjected to electric shock torture.

Many prisoners have died under interrogation, while others have suffered permanent impairments such as deafness after severe beatings about the head. Details are difficult to ascertain, especially since the Afghan government not only prohibited Western journalists from the country but said that they would be 'eliminated'. A French television reporter, Jacques Abouchar, was arrested by Soviet troops in October 1984 under the new law and sentenced to 18 years' imprisonment for working with the guerrillas, but was shortly afterwards 'pardoned' and released, so how hard the Karmal government seriously intends to pursue this policy remains in doubt. It seems likely that the Soviet government — which, after all, has seen several changes in its leadership since the invasion of Afghanistan, and is undoubtedly conscious of global criticism – is attempting to subdue Karmal's worst public excesses.

Working hand in hand with the *Khad* are the People's Revolutionary Tribunals which recall the worst excesses of the Red Guard terror in China and which have the power to sentence people to death for 'anti-government activities'. There is no right of appeal against such sentences, and the onus is upon the defendant to prove his innocence rather than upon the prosecution to prove his guilt. Moreover, the number of people being sentenced is increasing dramatically.

Khad suffers — fortunately — from limitations in its ability to infiltrate the guerrillas who keep the war against the Soviet invasion and Karmal's government alive. Because of their insular, tribal and religious composition, friends and allies within the guerrilla groups are well known and strangers are automatically suspect. This, coupled with the nature of the terrain in which they are fighting, is their greatest defence, and will ultimately — in my conviction — bring to the Soviet army the same humiliation the colonial French and then American forces found in Indo-China.

China

During the euphoria of a year in which HRH The Prince and Princess of Wales were scheduled (at the time of writing) to visit China, a closer look at the Ministry of Public Security which will guard them is clearly called for. Before that, however, it would be well to recall how the present People's Republic came into being, and why highly repressive methods of controlling dissidence are still considered necessary.

During the 19th century the commercial concerns of Europe — of Britain, of Germany, and of other countries — had sought, in their own words, to 'modernize' the country and introduce the 'benefits' of industrialization while simultaneously reaping a rich reward from the trade in opium. Conservatives in China objected to this western encroachment, leading to the succession of 'opium wars' in which General Charles 'Chinese' Gordon — the Victorian religious fanatic, alcoholic and homosexual who was later killed at Khartoum — played such a significant part.

Into this arena, in 1896, stepped publicly for the first time the 'Chinese Lenin', Sun Yat-sen, founder of the secret *Hsing Chung Hui* society whose aim was the overthrow of the imperial government and the 'Dragon Throne' of the Manchus, last bastion of a ruling class which had dominated China for 3,000 years. Kidnapped by Chinese secret police in London, Dr Sun succeeded in escaping from the Chinese Legation by throwing messages wrapped around half-crowns (now obsolete, but in those days valuable, coins) from his cell window which eventually found their way to the British police. The incumbent Prime Minister, Lord Salisbury, had him freed — the alternative would have been for Dr Sun to have been returned manacled to China to face torture and execution for having dared to challenge the ruling hierarchy. Sun Yat-sen returned to China instead a free man and established a republic in the province of Nanking following the death of the Dowager-Empress Tzu Hsi in 1908 and the accession of a two-year-old monarch, Pu Yi. This republic found such a popular following that within two months the Manchu dynasty had abdicated, leaving a power vacuum into which a young peasant farmer named Mao Tse-tung, then aged only

15, would soon step.

During the period of the First World War in Europe, fortunes hung in the balance in China, and by 1920 four warlords had emerged, medieval-style, as the real rulers — even though they were all at war with each other. This situation provoked the sadly cynical remark from Dr Sun — who by this time was besieged with his followers in Canton — that 'well-organized nations count votes out of ballot boxes. Badly organized nations count bodies, dead ones, on the battlefield.'

Sun appealed to first Britain and then America for help, but was turned down. In desperation, in 1923, he went to Stalin, who welcomed him with open arms and lent him the services of Michael Borodin together with military advisers, and also sold him arms with which to create out of the *Kuomintang* (KMT, or People's Party) a truly Leninist form of government. Heavily involved in this — he became responsible for the Chinese communist military academy at Whampoa — was Dr Sun's brother-in-law (at the time another nonentity) called Chiang Kai-shek.

By 1924, a year before he died, Dr Sun had in effect established himself as another warlord, with some 600,000 members in the KMT. Then came the first of several major ideological clashes within the ranks of the Chinese communist party. Chiang Kai-shek, who adopted Sun's mantle, believed that the revolution should emerge from the small but growing numbers of the Chinese middle-class, while Mao Tse-tung and others believed it should grow from the peasantry. However, as in all nations, the peasants were more conservative and property-conscious than those better-educated, and Stalin (who had experienced the same problem in Russia) supported the Chiang Kai-shek line, which was basically nationalist rather than communist, although it was designed to replace Chinese feudalism with a more modern, representative, form of government.

During the second half of the 1920s a series of brilliant military campaigns subdued the four major warlords and established Chiang as the country's premier. Now, however, he turned against the workers who had combined to support him, preferring the backing of the employers and bankers, and in Shanghai the army hunted down and shot the well-organized factory workers. It marked the beginning of the parting of the ways between Chiang and Mao and the end of Soviet support for the former.

Mao was a romantic and a cultural nationalist who, like Hitler in Germany, turned to his country's legendary past for ideals with which to unite the peasants behind him, form his own army, and become in his turn the ultimate warlord. After the abortive revolt in Hunan province which was quashed by the army, Mao resorted to hit-and-run guerrilla tactics, operating out of the mountains. His army to begin with was hardly impressive, consisting of around 1,000 peasants and 600 hill bandits, but it grew, and by 1930 Mao had established his own secret police force designed both to intimidate and to extract information from those opposed to him. Their methods at the time were just the same as those of the hill bandits, about whom Chiang Kai-shek's government said in an official report: 'When they capture a person . . . they first pierce his legs with iron wire and bind them together as fish are hung on a string. When they return to their dens the captives are interrogated and cut with sickles . . . Any who hesitate are immediately cut in two at the waist, as a warning to others.'

All over China, hundreds of thousands suffered and died as the government forces fought to control not just Mao's rapidly growing followers (by 1930 he controlled some five million people in five provinces) but also the other remaining warlords. The closest European parallel to the state of China at this time is probably the Thirty Years' War of the 17th century. Unification, as so often happens throughout history, would only come when the people found a common enemy.

In Japan, the effect of the 1930 London Naval Treaty, which a weak-willed Labour government signed to pacify the Americans (then at the height of their isolationist policy), coupled with economic tariffs against Japanese goods imposed by both Britain and America, was to produce a military coup. With Britain and America effectively powerless to intervene, the Japanese invaded Manchuria. The Chinese communist forces, which by 1934 were on the point of being defeated by Chiang Kai-shek, embarked upon what has entered history as the legendary 'long march' and headed north to repel the invader. Stalin persuaded the two warlords to band together against the common enemy.

To begin with, the comparatively sophisticated Japanese army seemed invincible, and the Chinese capital, Nanking, fell in December 1937. Reprisals against the civilian population were atrocious — over 20,000 people were gunned down or bayoneted in a massacre rivalled later only by Russian and German war crimes. But Japanese resources were being overstretched by the campaign. At home, ordinary people were starving, and supplying the army was a burden neither the economy nor the new constitution could bear without serious civil disturbance. By 1940, Japan had 'conquered' China in the traditional sense of occupying all the major cities, but both demography and geography were against them. The country was too large and its population too vast ever to be controlled properly by an occupying power. While maintaining a force in China, therefore, the militaristic and totalitarian government of General Eiki Tojo turned its attention towards Indo-China and the East Indies, provoking the war against America and the Allies which was to prove so devastatingly fatal.

To begin with, both Chiang Kai-shek and Mao Tse-tung fought together on the Allied side against the Japanese. However, the rift was growing and, after Chiang's forces murdered some 9,000 of Mao's followers in 1941, the two leaders pursued what were effectively independent campaigns against the Japanese. Both the Russians and the Americans sought to bring the two parties together again (despite the betrayal at Yalta which let the Soviets into Manchuria and sparked off the continuing Sino-Soviet territorial dispute). Mao was enthusiastic about working together to create a new China after the final expulsion of the Japanese invaders, but would not subordinate himself to Chiang's command — understandably, since he would probably have lost his head!

Thus, at the end of the Second World War, the stage was set for a resurrection of the power struggle between the two — a struggle which resulted in a four-year civil war. As before, Mao controlled the north and Chiang the south. To begin with Chiang looked like winning. He had the greater manpower and the largest financial resources. Unfortunately, inflation dwindled his reserves while, especially after the battle of Hsuchow in 1948, the size of his army dwindled too. Mao's followers in the meanwhile were increasing steadily, and the end result of the civil war was a victory for his Chinese communist party and the exile of Chiang to the island of Formosa (now Taiwan) where for some years he maintained an American-backed opposition government.

On the mainland, Mao solidified his power base in a purge which climinated an estimated two million people. He was then lured by Stalin into the Korean War — a pointless, useless conflict which resulted in a quarter of a million needless Chinese deaths. However, it was in Korea that the Chinese military police and security forces first experimented successfully with the 'brainwashing' techniques which would later be applied to the country's entire population.

Brainwashing in itself — defined as any technique used to alter a victim's memory or attitudes, or to remove knowledge or concepts from his consciousness — is not new. Ordinary torture can produce a change in attitude: a standpoint no longer remains tenable after a certain pain threshold has been passed. In other words, submission to what the torturer/interrogator wishes becomes preferable to continued agony, and a forced confession will be signed. Friends, relatives and slight acquaintances will be implicated. After a while, the average person can even rationalize his or her 'confession' and believe in its truth. After all, everyone does this to a greater or lesser degree almost every day that passes. We convince ourselves that what we have done is right even though our subconscious says 'no', and eventually we believe the false facts completely. The process is not always deliberate. The man whose courage breaks on the battlefield, causing him to flee, will rationalize and come to believe that he was really running for assistance. The man whose wife throws him out because he came home drunk once too often will convince himself that he would not have 'needed' a drink if she had not driven him to it. The child who finds a coin or a toy will say it was a 'present' and will come to believe it.

What the Chinese military psychologists did, learning both from their own culture's tradition of torture and its widespread use of opiates, and from the techniques pioneered by Pavlov used in Russia and wartime Germany, was to refine the techniques of 'persuasion' in order to take advantage of the human mind's need to rationalize and justify itself to itself, so that a hardened American combat veteran, for example, could 'genuinely' come to believe that he opposed the war and supported communism.

The basic strategy behind all forms of brainwashing is quite simple. Disorientate your subject, divorce him from all he knows is real, and induce a willingness to cooperate in the hope that some form of sense and stability will be re-established. Physical means can produce this state of mind. Putting someone in a freezing cold, wet, totally dark cell and bombarding his ears with 'white noise' from loudspeakers will produce a total state of disorientation after a while and the victim will hardly be aware of what he is saying when he is interrogated — particularly when drugs are used as well.

Two classes of drugs are principally used during modern brainwashing and interrogation — hallucinogenics and tranquillizers. Sometimes the two are mixed dangerously with stimulants. For example, if an interrogator is in a hurry he could begin by injecting the victim with sodium-amytal or an equivalent, causing drowsiness and loss of awareness of passing time. The same drug also produces sensory distortion and vivid wide-awake dreams. If it is followed by an injection of benzedrine or pervitine — both stimulants — the effect is similar to that of a stiff drink to a man with a bad hangover: he comes wide awake again with whatever is principally on his mind fighting for vocal expression. Prisoners so treated generally babble uncontrollably about those facts they most desperately want to conceal *because* those facts are in the forefront of their minds. There is a simple experiment anyone can try — without the use of drugs — which will show clearly how this works. Try *not* to think of something. Tell yourself 'I will not think of Chinese brainwashing for the next ten minutes'. I guarantee you will fail and every glance at the clock will prove me right!

Brainwashing, as opposed to interrogation, is a much slower process, and depends on a slow erosion of a subject's independence and will to resist. Anger, the psyche's normal protective shield when basic precepts are threatened, is subdued by the use of drugs such as haloperidol, aminazin or triftazin (known as neuroleptics). Widely used by doctors in psychiatric hospitals, if administered in large doses such drugs not only produce total mental docility — a state of mind in which subtle propaganda can change basic attitudes without the victim noticing — but also various physical side-effects such as jaundice, a form of Parkinson's disease, muscular wasting and reduced blood pressure. (See the chapter on the Soviet Union for

This man awaits execution in China, 1983

further details.)

Successes using such techniques on American, British and Common-wealth troops in Korea encouraged Mao to begin a nationwide brainwashing campaign which went under the euphemistic title of 'thought control'. His intent was to replace traditional Chinese values of loyalty to the family first and foremost with new ones of loyalty and total subservience to the state. Within five years it was obvious that Mao's programme was not working, so he tried a new ploy. In 1956 he announced 'let a hundred flowers bloom', opening — on the surface — the doors to a proper democratic debate. In fact what happened was that those who attempted to introduce reform had their names noted by secret police infiltrators and informers, and were arrested. It became egalitarianism gone mad. Many of the country's best brains found themselves demoted from positions of responsibility to sweeping the roads or cleaning out lavatories, while those with little ability found themselves in positions of authority they could neither understand nor control. The Soviet leader Nikita Kruschev said (in 1958) that in his attempt to force communism upon his people Mao was 'acting like a lunatic on a throne and turning his country upside-down'. Both Chinese agriculture and industry floundered to a virtual standstill within a year. Millions of people died, foreign revenue became non-existent, and Mao's godlike pedestal began to wobble.

From 1959 onwards a power struggle emerged between Mao, his actress wife Chiang-Ching, the head of state Liu Shao-chi and the army commander, Lin Piao. Until the mid-1960s this simmered under the surface of the so-called 'Cultural Revolution', which began as a questioning of Chinese artistic values and gradually came to permeate every facet of everyday life, down to such trivia as whether certain words were suitable for use by good communists. The 'student revolt' which would hit America and Britain during the second half of the decade had already begun in China when, in 1957–58, the first Red Guards appeared among the teenage schoolchildren of Tsinghua. Encouraged by Chiang-Ching, who stated 'Chairman Mao often says there is no construction without destruction', a wave of sheer vandalism directed against school and university authorities and academics in general swept the country. The 'Cultural Revolution' is often quoted as having been an intellectual revolt: it was the opposite. Teachers were lynched in the streets and schools were burned. Gradually, more and more targets came under attack. Someone wearing western-style clothes could literally have them torn from his back in the street. A girl with an elaborate coiffure could have her head shaved. Anything 'decadent' became fair game for the Red Guards, from shop window displays to restaurant menus. Worse, as far as China's economic development went, were attacks on scientists and technicians. Libraries were ransacked and thousands of books burned. The authorities were powerless to stop the

Chiang-Ching, Mao's widow during the Gang of Four trials.

rampage, far worse than anything which could even have been conceived by Ernst Röhm's brown-shirted stormtroopers in pre-war Germany. Private homes were broken into for evidence of 'capitalist' tendencies. Hundreds of thousands of people — perhaps as many as half a million — lost their lives or were thrown into stinking, cold jails, including Liu Shao-chi.

Chiang-Ching led the revolution from the top, addressing rallies and denouncing all things modern or western, from pop music to abstract art. She took over control of newspapers, radio and television stations, and all forms of free expression were prohibited. By 1967, however, the revolution had reached its climax. With the country in a state of virtual civil war, Mao finally withdrew his support from the Red Guards and used the army to restore order. Four years later, the army itself came under attack. Its commander, Lin Piao, was murdered, accused of conspiring to assassinate Mao, and there was a purge of senior officers. But the Mao era was almost over. He was suffering from Parkinson's disease, he had quarrelled with Chiang-Ching, and the couple separated in 1973. Mao's old comrade, Chou En-lai, was dying of cancer. Both men died in 1976, Chou in April and Mao in September.

For a few months the country was ruled by the so-called 'gang of four', comprising Chiang-Ching herself, Hua Kuo-feng, Wang Hun-wen and Yeh Chien-ying, but all four were arrested and jailed, later to be tried for national betrayal and sentenced to death. Teng Hsaio-ping emerged as the new leader. To most people he breathed a new air of sanity into the country. He had been a bitter opponent of the Cultural Revolution and abhorred the excesses of the Red Guards as well as the 'proletarian art' which Chiang-Ching had tried to introduce. He called for a return to common sense and moderation, returned the country to democracy, introduced curbs on civil service powers, restored the schools and reopened the libraries and museums.

However, with its vast and volatile populace, the Chinese government still needs a means of keeping a check on trends, particularly political trends, so that any further revolution can be nipped in the bud. The principal instrument in this is the Ministry of Public Tranquillity, with headquarters in Beijing (Peking). It has three principal departments: Unit 8341, responsible for the security of government officials and broadly comparable to America's Secret Service; the Internal Department, which is responsible for domestic security and for keeping an eye on Chinese political dissidents; and the External Department, responsible for foreign intelligence and counter-intelligence and for monitoring the activities of overseas visitors to China.

Regrettably, although torture has been officially prohibited in China since the mid-1950s, it is still used during the interrogation of political suspects and as punishment for detainees who break prison regulations. Chinese interrogation techniques will be familiar to anyone who has read any accounts of the treatment of American prisoners during the Vietnam War, and include severe beatings, partial suffocation, immersion in water, solitary confinement in either freezing cold or baking hot concrete cells and — for those suspected of espionage — the use of drugs, as described earlier. Chinese officials will not, of course, admit to the use of such methods, but they do justify the continuing use of the death penalty by pointing to the decline in the crime rate over recent years. However, no figures for the numbers executed are ever published.

The security services are particularly active in the north of the country, where a Buddhist separatist movement in Tibet has been causing the Chinese government concern, despite its totally non-violent nature. Some 30 people were arrested in Lhasa in August and September 1983 and are believed to be still held in prison. They include Buddhist monks. Ironically, in November 1984 the Ministry of Public Tranquillity issued a statement saying there are 'no political prisoners or "so-called" political dissidents in China . . .'

India

Queen Victoria's 'jewel in the crown' is, by any standards, severely flawed and the state of the nation today would have appalled Mahatma Gandhi and Jawaharlal Nehru, even though their own pacifist stands caused the loss of thousands of lives. In one of its most severe indictments of any country, Amnesty International has the following to say: 'Police brutality and torture have long been common and widespread in India and have continued . . . [AI] was concerned about the detention of prisoners of conscience and about large numbers of other political detainees who were held without trial under preventive detention legislation or who were awaiting trial under special legislation permitting trial *in camera*. It was also concerned about allegations of torture, in several cases reportedly resulting in death in custody; and about reports that alleged extremists were shot dead by security forces personnel after capture.'

The problem that India faces — and has always faced — can be readily summarized: 250 million Hindus, 90 million Muslims, 6 million Sikhs, uncounted members of other sects, both Buddhist and Christian; 23 languages and 200 dialects; and 3,000 castes — a social, racial, cultural and religious curry too hot for any palate. Gandhi could not solve India's problems nor could Nehru (who, coincidentally, was jailed for similar activities during exactly the same period that Hitler was incarcerated in Landsberg). The two 'greatest' figures in modern Indian history were shamans who led an over-populated, undernourished sub-continent through civil war in which half a million people died, through two disastrous wars against neighbouring Pakistan, through another war with China, into continuing civil war with ethnic minority groups. In such a climate do secret police forces flourish . . . but in India there is no 'secret' police, there is just the ordinary police: however, the *Gestapo* and *Sicherheitsdienst* would have relished their powers.

'I was taken to Mulug police station', relates one survivor of the break-away Indian communist Naxalite movement. 'In the evening at about 8:00 pm the police came. We [the man and four other prisoners] were all put into the police van. We were taken into the midst of the forest. We were made to get down from the van and we were taken about a mile to walk. Then the [police Sub-Inspector] addressed me: "At least even now divulge the truth". I was kept there. The remaining four people were taken to a distance of 50 feet and were tied to trees by ropes from foot to chest, with handcuffs on. A black cloth was tied over my eyes. The other four were also blindfolded. I heard [the Sub-Inspector] directing to fire. I heard one of them [the police] refusing to "fire". Thereupon the [Sub-Inspector] abused him in English. The people who were tied were raising slogans — "Long live Mao. Long live the revolution." I heard the firing of guns six times. Then [the Sub-Inspector] approached me and said "You lucky bastard, you are still alive". I was still blindfolded. After I was put in the van my blindfold was removed and I happened to look out and I found those four people with their heads hanging. Then I saw their ropes being removed and the four dead bodies were taken away in a Jeep. I was warned not to disclose this incident to anybody otherwise I will be shot dead like the other four . . .'

The reason for this witness remaining anonymous is obvious. The incident actually happened in 1975, but similar occurrences are still common. Following the assassination of Mrs Indira Gandhi, nearly 3,000 Sikhs were *officially* stated to have been killed (my italics — the actual figure is certainly far higher). Her successor, Rajiv Gandhi, publicly announced that the killings were to stop. But they have not. Nor are Sikhs who wish for — I was about to say 'seek' — independence the only victims of a vicious semi-totalitarian regime.

An almost unique method employed by the Indian police and security forces when they know or suspect someone is engaged in political activities hostile to the government is the staged 'shoot-out'. A former Chief Justice and head of the Punjab Police Commission, Meherchand Mahajan, stated that 'Considerable evidence has been led to the effect that police make out false encounters with criminals and shoot them because they cannot obtain sufficient evidence against them to bring them to justice before the courts of law . . . A number of witnesses suggested that when the police catch hold of dacoits* and can obtain no evidence against them, they tie them to trees and just liquidate them.' Such 'encounter' killings are, in a way, a natural police reaction to the wave of Naxalite killings of policemen since

*Dacoit — a word meaning a member of a group of five or more robbers or bandits.

the late 1960s in West Bengal and, in particular, in Andhra Pradesh.

A continually difficult question to answer in dealing with a subject of this nature is, 'do the ends justify the means?', whether those being killed or tortured are policemen or guerrillas, 'freedom fighters' or terrorists. Here, the Indian government under successive leaders has clearly adopted the attitude that terrorist methods will be countered by terrorist methods — and if the innocent suffer, as they do, daily, then so be it. My own view is that if a government is genuinely democratic and representative of a majority of its peoples' wishes, then those who wish to change it should do so by democratic means. Those who resort to violence, particularly indiscriminate violence against unsuspecting and innocent victims such as children, should be shown no leniency. However, if a government is not fully representative, and does not permit democratic methods to effect change, then I can see the argument that people must take the law into their own hands. The trouble with this is that it still leads to loss of innocent life — but a policeman cannot back away from a murderer who is holding a hostage, whether the motive for the kidnap is criminal or political.

The case of India is a particularly difficult one because no government can ever fully represent so many peoples of diverse backgrounds and beliefs, but it is still impossible to applaud or even sanction police methods which led, for example, to the following incident.

Shambynath Shaha was said by the Indian police to have been a Naxalite — his politics are certainly 'left wing'. In November 1970 he was arrested by the Calcutta police and tortured to make him reveal the names of his associates. When he proved obdurate he was taken, handcuffed, by car into the countryside where he was shot three times. Still alive and somehow conscious, he was taken to the bank of the River Ganges and shot twice more (a further shot missed). Why he was not then thrown into the river he will never know. Instead, he was taken to a third location — he does not know where because he was by this time unconscious — and shot a sixth time. His body was then dumped at the Marwari Relief Society Hospital. However, when the police returned to recover his corpse in the morning he was miraculously still alive, having been operated upon. The police later claimed that he had been inadvertently shot during an encounter with terrorists . . . but gave the date as one day later than that of his arrest.

The Indian police have a marvellous 'out' for the shooting of suspects who may or may not be terrorists. A Suppression of Disturbances Act dating back to 1948 gives the police powers to designate 'disturbed areas' and to 'fire upon, order fire to be opened or otherwise use force, even to the causing of death' on anybody inside such an area 'acting in contravention of any law or order for the time being in force'. Indian lawyers acting on behalf of Naxalites, Sikhs and others accused of conspiring against the government have reported numerous stories of people being arrested and

Sihk leader, Hindranwals, faced a standing order for his arrest.

Amritsar's Golden Temple damaged during the June 1984 battle between Sihk extremists and army troops.

then driven into 'disturbed areas' so they could be shot without any questions being asked.

'War', it has been said, 'is controlled violence', and perhaps the biggest problem in India is that the police and military are not sufficiently controlled. Certainly it is difficult to justify events following the 5 June 1984 shoot-out at the Golden Temple of Amritsar, the holiest Sikh shrine in the Punjab. Sant Jarnail Singh Bhindranwale, the extremist Sikh leader who had been responsible for provoking much of the violence in the Punjab over recent years, was killed together with nearly 500 followers (some of whom may have been innocent). Nearly 100 soldiers also died in the encounter, which received worldwide television news coverage. What was not so widely reported, however, was the subsequent arrest and detention of four women and 22 children — aged between *one* and 16 — who had been visiting the shrine at the time! They were not tortured, but many other people have been and continue to be, beatings, burnings with cigarettes, having fingernails torn out and being suspended by the ankles for hours on end being some of the favourite police methods.

In common with the governments of many other countries, that of India has refused to grant visas to members of international human rights groups seeking to conduct their own investigations . . .

Indonesia

The island state of Indonesia has been in turmoil ever since the end of the Second World War, principally due to the activities of the Indonesian Communist Party (PKI) and to guerrilla violence from those seeking the independence of East Timor (the *Frente Revolucionaria do Timor Leste Independente* or *Fretilin*) and those seeking the same for Papua (the *Organisasi Papua Merdeka*). Under these combined threats the governments of President Sukarno and his successor, General Suharto, have conducted a continuing military and paramilitary campaign for the last 20 years which shows no signs of ending.

The principal Indonesian security forces are the *Kommando Operasi Pemulihan Keamanan dan Ketertiban* (KOPKAMTIB), or Command for the Restoration of Security and Order, which is the real secret police force; *Intel*, or army intelligence; and the crack SAS-trained 'red berets' of the *Resimen Para Kommando Angkatan Darat* (RPKAD), or Parachute Assault Regiment.

During the 1960s the principal threat to President Sukarno's regime was seen as the communist PKI party, even though it had repeatedly stated its peaceful, non-revolutionary intentions. In 1965 the PKI was linked — probably with no justification — to an attempted coup by dissident army officers to overthrow the government, and General Suharto, on behalf of President Sukarno, acted with both speed and barbarity. The RPKAD paras were unleashed against an unsuspecting populace and a series of mass murders of PKI members or suspected members took place in which an estimated half a million people were eventually killed. The Amnesty International report, *Political Killings by Governments*, has the following horror story to tell.

'In the town of Kediri in Central Java, a PKI stronghold, some 7,000 PKI supporters are estimated to have been killed. In Banjuwangi in East Java, 4,000 people were killed in a few days. In East Java most people were executed with long sugar-cane knives and sickles; the slaughter often assumed a ritualistic and ceremonial character. In several places the killers held feasts with their bound victims present. After the meal each guest was invited to decapitate a prisoner — apparently to involve as many as possible in the killings.

'As the purge accelerated in November 1965 headless bodies covered with red flags were floated down rivers aboard rafts and heads placed upon bridges. Every day for several months riverside residents in Surabaya in East Java had to disentangle bodies that were caught on jetties. At one point so many bodies from Kediri filled the Brantas River that the downstream town of Jombang lodged a formal protest complaining that plague might break out. In the small mill town of Batu so many were executed within the narrow confines of a small police courtyard that it was decided it would be simpler to cover the piles of bodies with cement rather than bury the victims.'

Although the massacres have ceased, some 750,000 people were arrested at the time, and some are still serving prison sentences. Thirty-five are under sentence of death, although the government has given its word, informally, that the executions will not be carried out. Meanwhile, the three main branches of the security forces continue to seek out, arrest, torture and, in many cases, kill members of the two main nationalist organizations. Typical brutalities during interrogation include having matchsticks pushed under the fingernails then lighted; electric shock and suffocation treatment; severe beatings; and religious punishment, such as not allowing devout Muslims to pray, which is probably far more damaging mentally than any form of physical pain or humiliation.

Hundreds of people are in detention in security camps known as KODAKs throughout Indonesia, including Muslim leaders who organized a protest march against the continued incarceration of religious dissidents in 1984 (in which between 20 and 100 people were shot by the police). Others more 'rightly' detained include members of extremist Muslim groups, such as those responsible for the bomb attacks on branches of the Bank Central Asia in October 1984. In East Timor, where military operations continue, non-combatants suspected of aiding the guerrillas are frequently rounded up and executed. Despite requests from those seeking independence, and from international rights groups, for United Nations intervention in Indonesia, at the time of writing the civil war was still going on.

Kampuchea

Formerly known as Cambodia, Kampuchea succumbed to the communist forces of the *Khmer Rouge* in 1975. The Americans were expelled here as in Vietnam and a reign of terror against supporters of the previous government presided over by Lon Nol went into immediate effect. As readers of my previous book *The World's Elite Forces* will know well, the *Khmer Rouge* fought hard and without quarter, and their treatment of the civilian population of the country they now controlled was no less brutal and methodical. Whole cities, to which refugees had flocked during the war, were evacuated by force — often at only a few hours' notice — and their citizens forced to return to work as virtual slave labourers on the land. Supporters of the Lon Nol regime were ruthlessly hunted down and killed on the spot, as was anyone who questioned the new regime by word or deed. As in China during the Red Guard period, anyone suspected of being an 'intellectual' was persecuted and, in many cases, tortured and executed. Anyone wearing spectacles was automatically suspect and victimized, in much the same way as university students in British and American townships are frequently set upon by local thugs for no other reason than that they look like students.

The *Khmer Rouge* is a fanatical organization almost without parallel in modern history. Not only 'intellectuals' were persecuted: so also were ethnic minorities, especially the Vietnamese, Chinese, Laotian and Thai population; religious minorities such as the Muslim Cham; and anyone — particularly in the armed forces — who had served under the former regime. In the years following the *Khmer Rouge*'s victory, hundreds of thousands of people — the exact number is impossible to estimate – were killed in the most barbaric fashion.

This situation could not, and did not, last. In 1979 the so-called Government of Democratic Kampuchea was overthrown by the Kampuchean United Front of National Salvation after an invasion by Vietnamese troops, and today the country is divided into three warring provinces — supposedly forming a coalition government! The party of Democratic Kampuchea, or pDK, administers part of the country, the *Khmer* People's National Liberation Front, or KPNLF another; and the oddly named National United Front for an Independent, Neutral, Peaceful and Cooperative Cambodia (FUNCINPEC) the third. Unfortunately, there is little 'neutral, peaceful or cooperative' within the whole country. Each political administrative area maintains its own security forces and has established concentration camps for the detention of those holding opposing viewpoints. Thousands of people are kicked and beaten daily, subjected to political indoctrination

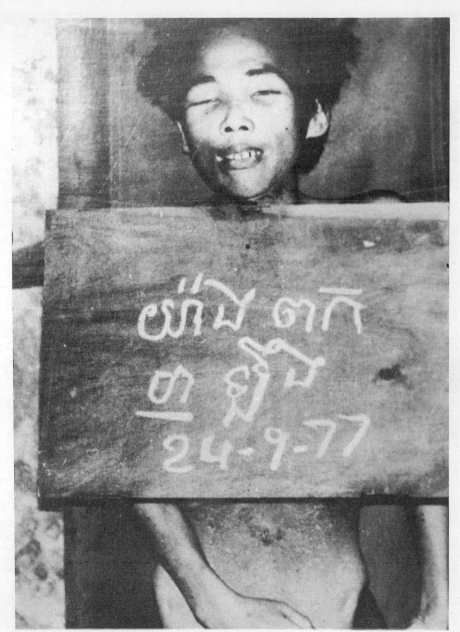

The corpse of a prisoner in Tuol Sleng prison.

Human remains excavated from a mass grave in Kampuchea, 1982.

talks and pushed into solitary confinement if they object. Many die from lack of food or medical care. Women are particularly vulnerable and group rapes by camp guards are commonplace.

The blame cannot be laid at the doors of any one 'secret police' service — there are too many, and the country has reached the stage where almost every man, woman and child is either a collaborator/informant, or in jail. It is an intolerable situation which the people themselves will resolve only by finally saying 'enough'.

Philippines

The Philippines, that group of Pacific islands with such romantic names over which the Japanese and Americans fought so fiercely some 50 years ago, and whose name alone conjures up such visions of tropical paradise is, in fact, a hell-hole of political, police and military corruption and sadism to rival the worst of what the rest of the world can offer. Under its president, Ferdinand Marcos, the security forces comprising the Military Intelligence and Security Group (MISG) and the Regional Security Units of the Philippine Constabulary (RSU PC2) have a virtually free hand to arrest, abuse, molest, beat, torture and kill anyone suspected of being in opposition to the government, from communists to religious leaders. Nor are tourists free of surveillance or the occasional 'unofficial' roughing-up if they inadvertently stray into a 'sensitive' area where a police operation is taking place.

The Philippines are a group of islands, the largest being Luzon and Mindanao, lying strategically between Japan and Indonesia/Malaysia and the route to Australia, which is why they became so important in the Second World War. In the immediate post-war period, the Philippines were to all intents and purposes an American colony, and the South-East Asia Treaty Organization document was actually signed in Manila, the islands' capital, in 1955. Why is the situation so different today?

In 1972 the terrorist activities of the Moro National Liberation Front — ethnic nationalists seeking independence from the Philippines — and the New People's Army, a communist organization, reached such a pitch that President Marcos was forced to declare martial law. This was maintained until 1980 but several of its provisions are still in force, such as the right of the police to put suspected terrorists in preventive detention and the suspension of *habeas corpus*. During the period of martial law several hundred people arrested by the security forces have never been seen again; others have eventually reappeared with horrifying descriptions of torture and conditions in President Marcos' detention camps. However, that the situation has not really improved can clearly be seen from the following testimony of a 24-year-old farmer, Wenifredo Villareal y Maravilla, who was arrested by men of the 3rd Military Police Brigade on 22 April 1985 while on a journey to visit relatives. He and a companion, Jaime Bas Morco, had

Relatives bury a young man murdered by Philippino secret police.

forgotten to put their identity papers in their pockets and, when the pass-
enger Jeep they were travelling in was stopped for a routine check, they
were immediately seized on suspicion of being members of the NPA. They
were taken to an interrogation centre at Mauraro.

'I was boxed and kicked many times on the stomach, struck with the
Armalite rifle's butt on the nape, my face was submerged in a toilet bowl
many times, my hands were tied with electric wire and was switched on an
electric outlet after which my penis was also applied with electric current
by tying it with live electric wire. My heart seemed to burst every time the
electric current flowed into my body. After electrocuting me, my penis was
applied with grinded hot peppers. One of my torturers found the "Vicks
Vapour Rub" in my pocket and it was emptied into my eyes, nose and
mouth, which nearly blinded me.

'I was forced to drink two litres of muddy water after which they boxed
me on the stomach many times which sent the muddy water spurting out
of my mouth. Another torturer of mine got an electrical plier and tried to
pull my fingernails. Fortunately my fingernails were cut short so they could
not pull my nails out of place. My face was covered with a wet towel for a
few minutes. My heart seemed to explode whenever I tried to gasp for
breath. Another soldier got a sharp knife and lightly slashed my throat
while saying, "If you do not confess that you are an NPA, I will bury this

blade in your stomach".

'I was brought outside the torture chamber and asked to bow into a ditch and was told, "If you do not confess, we will bury you right here". Changing their minds, I was again brought inside the torture chamber and was asked to stand up before a concrete wall with my hands spread sideways as if I was Jesus Christ nailed up on the cross. At that time my knees trembled, then I lost consciousness. I collapsed three times. I only regained consciousness when they poured a bucket of muddy water over me.'

After signing a 'confession', Wenifredo Villareal was transferred first to the Camp Villa Hermosa then on to Camp Bagong Ibalon, where he was detained until 4 June. Many hundreds of others have been similarly treated. On 24 March 1983 some 30 military personnel raided the house of a German Lutheran pastor in Davao City, Mindanao, where they arrested a Roman Catholic lay community worker, Hilda Narcisco. She was blindfolded and bundled into a car before being driven to a secret interrogation centre or 'safe house'. En route the soldiers molested her sexually, and during her interrogation the following day she was raped. On 26 March, still uncharged, she was sent to Camp Catitipan, outside Davao City. Relatives petitioning for her release finally got a judge to intervene, ordering charges of subversion to be dropped for lack of evidence, but she was not released until 6 September. Since then Hilda Narcisco has fought a vigorous campaign to get those responsible for molesting and raping her arrested, but has been unable to identify them due to lack of cooperation by the authorities.

Many other people have been similarly arrested and maltreated, including members of the *Kilusang Mayo Uno*, a trades union movement, and numbers of church workers. In May 1984, prior to a general election, conflict between the NPA — who are, it must be remembered, armed insurgents — and the security forces intensified. Shortly after polling, 11 men from the hamlet of Langoni were arrested by a Regional Security Unit of the Philippine Constabulary on suspicion of being NPA members. They were marched to the headquarters of the 338th Company of the PC where an eyewitness said they were kicked and beaten. Nine of them were subsequently shot and their mutilated bodies returned to their village the next day. The witness was himself charged with murder, although the case was later dropped. Other witnesses, in fear of their own lives, refused to testify before a military commission investigating the case so that none of the police responsible were ever charged. It will be interesting to see whether similar stories emerge now that the new Aquino administration has taken over from deposed President Marcos.

Sri Lanka

In Sri Lanka (formerly Ceylon) a state of emergency has existed since 1979 due to the extremist activities of Tamil guerrillas seeking an independent Tamil state on the island. Other groups in armed opposition to the government include the People's Liberation Front and the Sri Lanka Freedom Party, and hundreds of people have been arrested, tortured and in many cases killed by the military, by the Criminal Investigation Department (CID) or the Special Task Force, a recently formed counter-insurgency unit. The following affidavits reveal typical methods of the security forces in extracting information and 'confessions' from suspects.

1. 'While questioning me he now and then placed on my leg a device which made me feel that I was subjected to an electric shock. This he did five times. Every time . . . my whole body shook violently and I was in a state of shock. The device appeared to be about two and a half feet long and pipe-shaped, black in colour. At one end there was a coiled spring. At the other end was a switch which was pressed every time it was applied . . .'

2. 'I was put in a dark room, stripped of all my clothes and made to lie on the floor. My hands and feet were chained and large spikes were inserted into my body. I was assaulted with machine-guns, iron rods on the knee joints, neck region, close to the eyes, on the feet and almost all parts of my body. I was bound with chains on the legs and let down a deep well, then pulled up.'

3. 'On 2 December 1984 I was playing with my child in the compound of my house when a soldier armed with a rifle who came along called me to come out. This soldier then spoke to another soldier who was close by and then turned and fired at me. The bullet hit on the right side of my stomach, which pierced through and found an exit on the back close to the hips, leaving a gaping wound. I was then rushed to hospital. I did not commit any offence by playing in the compound of my house with my child and do not know why I was punished in such a manner.

4. 'I was stripped naked. A rope was tied around my ankles. I was dragged along the floor to the doorway and the rope around my ankles was passed through the wooden ventilation grille over the door. I was pulled up by my feet hanging upside down, facing the room with my head two or three inches off the ground. I was hit on the back upper part of my legs with plastic pipes . . . I was struck with iron rods on the soles of my feet. Then they brought burning coal and chillies on a tray. When they dropped the chillies on to the coal, the two interrogating officers had to leave the room from the smoke. A soldier then tied a sarong around my waist so that it fell down over my head like a funnel. The burning chillies were placed inside. Owing to the fumes, I felt a burning sensation. I had difficulty in breathing. I remained like that for two or three hours. I was untied and dropped to the ground. I lost consciousness.'

The Sinhalese Prevention of Terrorism Act of 1979 gives the government security forces wide powers of arrest and detention without trial, and as

Edwin Lopez, arrested and subjected to electric torture, Philippines, 1982.

can clearly be seen from the foregoing — particularly the incident where the young mother was shot apparently on a whim — this has led to excesses. While one cannot deny any government the legal right to protect itself against armed terrorism, there need to be controls on their powers in order to protect the innocent, and in Sri Lanka that is plainly not the case. Under the law, Sinhalese citizens have the right of complaint to the Supreme Court if police or army officials violate the International Covenant on Civil and Political Rights — to which the government is a signatory — but in practice most people fear reprisals against themselves or their families, and those who are prepared to give testimonies such as those quoted here will normally only do so anonymously.

Acknowledgements
The publisher thanks the
following organizations for
their kind permission to
reproduce the photographs in
this book:
Amnesty International 2–3, 4–5,
24, 27, 35, 36, 37, 44, 47, 73,
77, 80, 112, 125, 126, 137, 149,
150–151, 153, 156; John
Frost/Daily Mail 59; The
Photo Source 99, 139;
Popperfoto 12–13, 21,
100–101, 103, 129; Topham
17, 28, 31, 50–51, 54, 56–7,
105, 106, 110, 117, 120, 144–5,
145.